Binder Twine 'n Bandaids

Homegrown Humor from the Heartland

by D.D. Dunn

Goblin Fern Press, Inc.
Madison, Wisconsin
www.goblinfernpress.com

ISBN 0-9647663-2-9

Cover photo and other farm images in the book are
pictures of Dunn Movin' Farm,
taken the day we moved in, June 12, 1963.

Cover, book design and typography:
Printing Services Management, Inc.

Published by
Goblin Fern Press, Inc.
888-670-BOOK (2665) Madison, WI
www.goblinfernpress.com

Printed in the United States of America
Second printing: November 2003

This book is dedicated to my husband, Marc,
and to our children,
Elizabeth, Amy, Alicia, Amanda and Chad,
and to my mother, Jean.

Thanks
for the memories...

Acknowledgments

I thank God for keeping me in His loving care, for watching over me when I got in over my head, and for all the blessings He has bestowed—my family, my friends, my church and my life, and for the moments of time that left the memories I hold so dear.

I thank my husband, Marc, for all of his support and encouragement. For his willingness to do whatever needed to be done so I could go on with my mission. He is my hero, my partner, my strength and my best friend.

I thank Elizabeth for being willing to wait "a few minutes" to read a book, or to get a snack or to play the marble game, and for her making this project so much a part of daily life that she can now recite almost every story from memory.

I thank my grown children, Amy, Chad, Alicia and Amanda, and their spouses and their children, for understanding when I was so preoccupied with this venture that I neglected our time together. I thank them for gathering 'round the table after every holiday meal, and listening to the same old tales over and over throughout their childhood.

I thank my mom and dad. They taught me I could get by with a lot less if I need to, that wanting and getting are two different things, and that if I am willing to do the work, no goal is beyond my grasp.

I thank Dan and Cindie, friends who are more like family, always willing to share their time, opinions and encouragement. Friends who were willing to listen to my doubts, calm my fears and to hold me in their prayers every day.

I thank my brother, my two sisters and the folks who lived in our little town. Their participation in my life is the foundation for the memories I have to share. I changed your names, but I think you still know who you are.

I thank Janet from Printing Services Management, Inc.—her creative talent and ability to stop on a dime and change direction is remarkable. Her newfound friendship is a welcome bonus.

I thank Kira Henschel from Goblin Fern Press for being so patient and supportive during every step of this journey. I want to thank her staff for their hard work and their willingness to see this project through to its completion. They have all worked late and come in early to ensure the project's success. They made this undertaking enjoyable, exhilarating and rewarding.

And I don't want to leave out that guy who called trying to buy the book; he is the one who finally got the ball rolling.

Then, of course, there's you. All of you who read this, laugh out loud, and send me an email about how some of the same stuff happened to you. All of you who smile and nod your head while you read through the pages of my life. All of you who think you might have gone to the same school as me, and all of you who put out your hard earned money just to see what the book was about.

Thank you all,
from the bottom of my heart.

A note from the author...

Before I share my stories with you, I think it is important for you to understand that I am not the only storyteller in my family. We all tell 'em. My mom has her set, my brother and both my sisters have a pile all their own, and my dad had a big bunch of 'em, too. Every holiday, every birthday, every event that brought us all together, brought out the stories. We told 'em at weddings, and funerals, picnics and the times when we just all happened to show up at the same place at the same time.

These are the stories of our lives, our opportunity to be in the spotlight for a moment. I guess it's our way of letting you know how we turned out the way we did. In our family, when the whole brood was around and one of us was finishing up one of the tales, people would shout out a story they wanted to hear next. All of us know all the stories by heart, but it's always nice to hear them one more time from the "horse's mouth."

The stories have evolved over the years. Parts were left off or added on. And as my circle of friends grew, I started telling my stories in a broader market. I told them at Christmas parties, cookouts and get-togethers, pretty much anytime I couldn't think of anything else to say. I've changed the names of the people in the stories. My dad always said the difference between talk and gossip was whether or not your audience knew whom you were talking about. I didn't want to be a gossip.

Since I first started telling these stories, I've developed quite a reputation. People began repeating the stories to their circles of friends, and one day a stranger called, said he knew someone, who knew someone, who knew someone I knew, and he wanted to buy the book of my stories. He was disappointed to hear there was no book to buy. He started me thinkin', though. And the next cloudy summer day, I decided to sit down and try to write out one of the stories on paper. One after another, the piles began to grow, until pretty soon I had enough to fill a book!

So I did, and here it is. I hope you enjoy it!

D.D. Dunn
Davenport, IA

Table of Contents

CHAPTER ONE

Dunn-Movin' FARM

In 1963, my family moved to a small farm in western Illinois. I was seven, my brother Mark was sixteen, and Sharon, the next oldest, was eighteen and a senior in high school. Our oldest sister, Becky, had married and moved out of the house four years before, leaving Mom 'n Dad with us stragglers. We'd been living in a little blue house, one with lights and water, on a couple of acres of land in a little town about an hour away from our new place. A couple of months before the move, the state decided to buy our house to put in an interstate. The men in the black suits had come by our digs, given us a check and an eviction notice, and said we had to move on.

When my parents told us we were moving to a farm with woods and barns and animals, I was excited 'n rarin' to go. I had visions of my uncle's dairy farm in Wisconsin—lots of white barns with concrete floors, beautiful pastures filled with horses, and a big white house with a huge front porch that wrapped around the front and one side. My uncle had five daughters and all they did was play in the yard. They didn't have to do much work, it seemed to me. I decided that it would be an ideal situation and eagerly gathered up my stuff so I could go.

We loaded up our '53 International pickup truck, tied on all we could carry and headed for the hill country. It took a couple of trips to get everything moved, but we got it all out to the farm in a single day.

The first time we pulled up to our new place, I could tell right away it wasn't a dairy farm. There was a house, but...not exactly how I'd pictured it. The old ramshackle building was covered with green tarpaper and parts of the roof were falling in. There was only one cupboard in the kitchen, and the sink sat on top of it. A filthy stool stood in a closet off to one side. It looked like they tried their hand at indoor plumbing and gave up on the job about half way through.

There was no running water. The only electricity was one sagging wire that ran from a pole out in the yard to the basement to run a stoker for a coal furnace. The furnace was bigger than any of the bedrooms, and there was a trough where coal came into a big holding bin. There were no lights in the house, but I was pretty sure Mom 'n Dad had a plan to rectify that. They needed electricity to have their coffee and the news radio going in the mornings, so I was pretty sure Dad would be rigging up some sort of power pretty quick.

No human beings had lived in the house for more than 25 years. The steps to the upper level and the basement (I use that term loosely) had been removed to prevent the livestock from getting hurt. A hole in the kitchen wall about three feet wide had been left behind where a chimney had fallen in and there were certain places we weren't supposed to step because the floor might give way. The summer kitchen for the house was a separate building down at the bottom of the hill near the well, and the previous owners were storing hay out there. There were bales of hay stacked all around the house, and you could see tunnels in the sides of the bales where critters were making attempts to dig into the house for winter.

It just kept getting worse as I looked around. The tractor shed in front of the house was falling down, and I could see a few other sheds and shacks and a chicken coop in the gully that divided the farmhouse from the barn lot. Some trees had died and were leaning over, and you had to walk up a dirt path to get to the front door. Out in the barn lot was a boxcar, a corncrib and a weathered hay barn that was unsafe for animals, which is why they had been staying in the house. Little sheds for pigs filled up one lot, and it wasn't long before I started planning to make one of those my new clubhouse.

All the fences were either falling down or non-existent and there was junk everywhere. Rusty strips of barbed wire wove their way along fence rows and hung like lassos on the rotted fence posts. Parts of machines that must have died years ago, lots of pieces of the tin roof that had come off the barns, and heaps of broken boards lay before me.

There was so much stuff scattered around that my older brother, Mark, invented a game called "Island." You would travel from the house through the gully to the barn, stepping on pieces of junk (the islands) without touching land.

We had about 40 acres of tillable ground, 40 acres of woods, and the house, barn and garden—almost 90 acres of run-down, beat-up, piled-up junk. I couldn't believe we were moving there on purpose.

The kids in our family didn't live in a democracy; whatever my folks wanted is what we did. No kid ever got to vote. My parents loved that place, so all we could do was move in and make the best of it. My mom hung the family motto on the living room wall before we started to unload—"Use it up and wear it out, make it do or do without." Once she put up her sign, there was no going back.

I was the youngest so got last pick of the bedrooms; mine was the smallest one and had no closet. All I could do was haul in my stuff and set up shop.

That first year, we barely held on. We couldn't plant because it was too late in the season when we got there, so we bought a milk cow, some chickens, and lots of sheep and pigs. Then we began putting up fences so the animals could go down in the woods and eat.

We were lucky Dad had a job at a nearby factory or we could have starved to death. He worked nights as a tractor repairman, came home and slept a few hours, then got up to farm until it was time to head back into town and work for some real money. I don't know how he did it all those years, but he managed. He left for work before we got home from school, and was always up and out doing chores before we got up in the morning. I think he was powered by caffeine and nicotine and biscuits 'n gravy. He was a tall, skinny fellow with huge hands and blue eyes, a tender heart and an infectious laugh. I loved my dad; he was my hero. I figured if he wanted to live out at this place, it must be the right place for us, even though the farm seemed to need everything, well, everything except binder twine.

We had an abundance of binder twine. It was in the house, in the yard, in every barn and shed and hanging from every tree.

The thick, bristly cord torn from the old bales of hay was a godsend. We used it to wrangle wayward sheep, tie the bumper back onto the truck, hang our clothes out to dry, and keep the screen door from flapping in the breeze.

Binder twine is indestructible. You can't break it, you can't cut it, and I don't even think you can get the stuff to burn.

Binder twine held the gates open and the bathroom door shut. It held pictures to the walls and kept sheep out of the garden. We used it to fill mouse holes in the floors, figuring it would take the little buggers a while to chew through that stuff. Binder twine held the propane tank to the wall for the old gas stove and kept our curtains hanging over the windows. If anything anywhere needed to be restrained, binder twine came to the rescue.

Binder twine did have its bad points, though. Animals were always getting tangled up in it. It would lie in wait for a mower, then grab onto the blade and twist it up like a corkscrew. It loved to see a kid running through the grass, then grab an ankle, and pull the runner face down in the dirt. Binder twine is ruthless. You have to have respect for the beast.

Yep, binder twine 'n bandaids kept us going. In fact, if you happen to be driving a red '64 Ford pickup, pop the hood and check out the wires going to the starter. If they have been spliced and are wrapped with bandaids, you might be driving our old truck. We kept a good supply of bandaids around the place, in the house and out in the tool shed, and even in the bins on the backs of the tractors. Somebody was always cutting their knuckles, or getting caught up in the barbed wire. We needed plenty of bandaids. They were always at the top of our grocery list. We made our own bread to save money, but always seemed to have some kind of trust fund available to keep us in good with the bandaid companies.

Even with our storehouse of necessities, my mother wasn't totally satisfied. She was mad that the barn had running water and the house didn't. We kids had to carry ten-gallon galvanized buckets of water into the house each morning so she could cook, clean and wash us. Once the water made it into the house, there was an added bonus. We could use the toilet! We'd pour water down the tank, and flush it down the drain into a cistern. Things were looking up.

I remember my Dad nailing an old wooden extension ladder to the upstairs landing so we could go upstairs to the bedrooms. He did the same thing for the basement dungeon so we could throw coal in the furnace. When the church in the near-by town burned down, Dad got a set of steps out of the rubble and we could go up 'n down stairs like regular folks.

By the time winter set in, Dad had rigged up some electric outlets, three on the main floor and one for a light in the upstairs hallway. The whole family was happy about that. We still had to carry water, but at least at night we could watch TV.

We became drop-cord junkies. We couldn't get enough drop-cords. We ran extension cords from the three electric outlets to every room in our house. (We were forbidden to run a drop-cord from the one plug on the back porch; it was for the freezer only.) The hallway light upstairs never had less than four drop-cords running from it. Dad changed fuses as fast as we could plug in appliances.

From time to time, someone would swipe your drop-cord. Then there'd be a big to-do and lots of accusations until you located the culprit, retrieved your cord and got electricity back in your room. My dad was usually the guilty party. He always needed everybody's drop-cords. Seemed he had an issue with us overloading the fuses and trying to burn down the house.

The next spring, as soon as the weather got warmer, we dug a trench from the well at the bottom of the hill to the house. Come fall, we had a real sink, some wooden cabinets, and running water. In the meantime, Sharon had graduated from high school and moved out on her own up near Chicago. She'd found a job working for the airlines and was living a glamorous life in her own apartment in the big city. Mark would stay on the farm another year until he finished school and left the comforts of home.

These are the stories that came from living on that farm, from being raised in a place where things were simple. These are the stories of living and learning life's lessons on the place my folks called "Dunn-movin" Farm.

CHAPTER TWO

Beggin' for DONUTS

Sometimes my mouth engages before my brain kicks in. It's happened to me more than once. It happened quite a bit when I was growing up on the farm, and still does now and then.

One particular evening, when I was about seven years old, Dad rounded up the family and announced we were going to meet someone he knew from work. We kids had never met these folks before, and Daddy wanted to have all of his children get there while we were still cleaned up. All during the drive over to his friends' house, Dad gave us examples of how we should behave when we got there.

We were supposed to say, "Yes, Sir" and "Yes, M'am." We were not supposed to fight with each other or with any of their kids. He warned us that no one better stick anything up his or her nose, and for God's sake, "Flush the toilet if you use it." We were all equipped with everything we needed to be good guests. Just before we poured out of the car, Dad said if "ANYONE did ANYTHING to embarrass him, they'd get a whoopin'." He said he meant it, too. He had to add that part, because it was usually our mother who gave out the whoopings, not our dad, not ever. Dad was a big old softie.

As soon as we got there, we found out they had two children—a girl my sister's age and a boy a few years younger than my brother. They had no one anywhere close to my age, and no toys of any interest to a little girl.

The mom thought I was cute, though, or so she said, and she invited me to sit at the table in the kitchen and color in a brand-new coloring book while the adults visited and the other kids went upstairs. That was okay with me, because she offered me a fancy donut that the other kids weren't going to get. I sat down with my milk and my donut and began to color a picture of a big, beautiful butterfly.

Time passed. The adults played pinochle and ate peanuts. My brother, Mark, had already been smacked a couple of times for trying to get the other boy to taste coffee grounds and telling the kid to stick his tongue on the freezer shelf. (Even I was smart enough to know better than to try that, but that other boy apparently wasn't the sharpest tack in the box.) My sister Sharon was being yelled at for turning up the record player too loud, and for making too much noise hopping around upstairs. Dad said it sounded like the ceiling was going to fall in. I was being good, sitting at the kitchen table and coloring nicely, begging for more donuts each time the Mrs. came in the room.

Pretty soon, the Mrs. told me I couldn't have any more donuts. She told me that there were only two left, and she needed to save them for her husband's breakfast the next morning. She said they didn't get donuts very often either, and they were her husband's favorite kind. I said okay, and kept on coloring.

When the Mrs. came back to fill up the peanut bowl, I showed her how well I was coloring, told her how I'd done my very best job ever, and that I wanted her to have my masterpiece. I think I might have said I was still a little bit hungry, and if it would be okay if I just had half of one of the donuts left over in the box.

She said she thought I'd done a wonderful job on the butterfly and that she could understand how anyone who worked that hard might be famished, so she decided I could have one more whole donut. Let me point out right here that I didn't ask for a whole donut, just a little bit.

The clock was still ticking, the adults were still playing pinochle and eating peanuts, and it was getting late. Mark had been warned lots of times to stop pestering the kid without a brain. Sharon and the tall, skinny girl were playing with make-up and Mom had said they had better wash that gunk off or else someone would think it was Halloween. Dad mentioned that they'd better hold the noise to a low roar, and I was still being good, sitting at the kitchen table and coloring nicely, and begging for the last donut every time the Mrs. came in the room.

When my own mother finally came into check on me and noticed I'd eaten all but one of the donuts, she got very close to my face. Her tone started out like a whisper, but then switched to more of a low, deep growl. Anyway, it was a threat, and she said I'd best not be begging for that last donut or else she was going to make me hard-to-catch!

The Mrs. came in right then and caught her (whew, that was a close one). The Mrs. then said everything was fine, as long as there was one donut left for breakfast. Mom turned around and gave me the look. You all know exactly which one I mean. It's not the "I-will-kill-you-when-I-get-you-out-to-the-car" look, but the one just before that, more like the "You're-lucky-she-showed-up-when-she-did" version. Then Mom pointed at me with that one finger, and I smiled back, which might have been a mistake, because it forced her to raise one eyebrow. You don't want to mess with my mom when she has given you the "one-brow" warning. I knew I was treading on thin ice, but I liked to live dangerously.

Eventually the card game came to a close, kids were rounded up, and socks and shoes were located. Good-byes were handed out. All that "You must come again," "No, it's our turn to have you over," vague adult banter was traded about over my head.

Then the Mrs. turned to me and said, "You look tired, Doris. I bet you'll be glad to get home and climb into your own bed."

I saw my opportunity and I took it. "Yes, but I'll have to get somethin' to eat before bedtime. I'm soooooooo hungry! I wish I had one more donut!"

That forced my mother into the combat mode. She put her arm around my shoulder and gave me a hard squeeze. With one swift and experienced motion, she had me out the door, down the steps and headed toward the car. I turned and tried to give the starving puppy dog expression to the Mrs., so she'd see me before I was shoved out from under the light. Mom put her hand on the top of my head, whirled me back around and gave me one more shove. I let my shoulders drop, whipped up a few tears and let them start running down my face and off my nose. I needed more time, so I started dragging my feet and stumbling.

Just as I crawled into the car and took my place in the back seat between the two older kids, the Mrs. came to my aid.

She knocked on the window and Sharon rolled it down most of the way. The Mrs. was holding a napkin, and wrapped inside was the prize I'd been seeking—the last chocolate-glazed donut! The Mrs. explained that the Mr. had been putting on a few pounds and he really didn't need to have it for breakfast after all. She said she knew it was late, and small children do tend to get hungry waiting for those long card games to end.

It was a huge victory! Not only did I get the last donut, but—she handed it to Sharon and made her pass it over to me! Sharon and Mark didn't get one, just me. Ha-Ha.

Unfortunately, it became clear to me on the ride home that I'd bought the donut at a high price. I guess I hadn't seen the tag hanging there when I made the bid.

As soon as we pulled out of the driveway, both my mom and dad started yelling at once. They said how terrible it had been for me to talk this poor family out of their last donut. They were embarrassed that I acted like I'd never seen a donut before in my life. They reminded me that we'd eaten a big supper just before we left home. Dad said he should just pull the car over right there on the highway and give me a spanking! He kept yellin' 'n hollerin' about it and I knew the only way to save my hide was to take immediate action.

As soon as I finished eating my delicious, wonderful, chocolate-covered donut, I started to lean over with my head against Sharon's shoulder. After the appropriate time had passed, I began to breathe a little slower and louder so that everyone would think I was sleeping. When Sharon shoved me over to the opposite side, I let myself fall like a sack of potatoes. I kept my eyes closed and went limp.

It seemed like we traveled a long way, but sooner or later, I heard the car turn off the blacktop and onto our lane. I opened one eye just a slit once in a while to get a bearing on where we were along the road.

When Mark got out of the car, I fell all the way over in the seat, and let one arm dangle down to the floorboard of the car. I didn't want anyone to think I was even partially awake. After all, what parent would beat a sleeping child?

Dad walked around to the back door, took one look at me, and said, "She looks so sweet! She's sound asleep. I think we just stayed too late and she probably was hungry. Poor little thing."

Good news! Sounded like I might get away with "Operation Donut" after all!

"Just take her in and put her to bed on the couch." Mom was never one for carrying a kid up the stairs.

I snorted a little, half opened one eye, and put my arms around my daddy's neck. I knew that would be the clincher. No spanking for me tonight!

He gave me a little hug and patted my back. Yep, I knew how to keep my rear out of the wringer. Dad thought I was "sweet." He had forgotten all about the donuts. I was saved!

Out in the living room, Mom had taken off my shoes and socks, brought me one of her own pillows out of the bedroom, and tucked me in on the couch with one of Grandma's soft, old, heavy comforters.

The dim lights were spilling in on the carpet from the dining room, and I could hear the rest of the family getting ready for bed. Mom was telling everyone to be quiet so as not to wake me up. Not only had I gotten all the donuts, I didn't have to bring anything in from the car, I didn't have to wash up and I didn't have to get my 'jamas on. Oh yea! I was the big winner! I was having trouble not breaking into a loud laughing fit, so I turned over and faced the back of the couch. I didn't want to get caught smiling.

Just then, Sharon came in and turned on the television. Sharon invested a good part of her life trying to get me in trouble, and she was still at it that night. She flipped the channels until she found the Carol Burnett Show, a family favorite. It sounded funny, and I wanted to see what was going on. I rolled back over on my side, pulled the comforter down just low enough to peak out and started watching the show from over Sharon's shoulder. I might have even laughed out loud once or twice, though I'm not sure, but I might have. Maybe. But I don't think I did.

Anyway, Mom came into the living room and told Sharon she had to turn off the TV because I was asleep on the couch.

"No, she isn't. I heard her laugh. She's awake!" Sharon was such a big, fat tattletale! I thought that I'd better get this cleared up straight away or she was going to blow my cover.

I pulled the blanket back over my head, and said in a clear voice, "I am not awake. I was asleep before we even got out of town!"

As soon as the words left my mouth, I knew I'd made a grave error in judgment. I was pretty sure a sleeping child would not have said that, so I tried to cover my tracks. I let the blanket fall to the floor, rubbed my eyes and asked, "Who said that?"

Mom and Dad were both standing right beside the couch and they didn't buy the act.

I got in trouble for eating the donuts. I got in trouble for pretending to be asleep. I got in trouble for letting Dad carry me in all the way from the car. I got in trouble for watching TV. I had to clean up and put on my 'jamas and go all the way upstairs to my room to go to bed, and I couldn't use Grandma's comforter either.

I was mad! Sharon was a big, fat tattletale! It was all Sharon's fault! She must be adopted, because if she were really one of us, she would never have ratted me out to the other side! I stomped my feet when I passed by Sharon on my way up the stairs. I glared at her when I went by. I tried to block the TV so she'd miss the best part of the show. I wanted her to know I was mad! She stuck her tongue out at me, and didn't look very happy either. Mom pointed at Sharon and raised one eyebrow.

Oh well, the night wasn't a total loss. I might have gotten the spanking, but at least I got the donuts, and now Sharon was walking on thin ice, too. When I reached the top of the stairs, I turned around and took my seat on the top step. I put my elbows on my knees, and made a cup with my hands to hold my chin. I decided it was worth the wait. Sooner or later, Sharon was going to get it. She'd already gotten the "one-brow" warning; now it was just a matter of time.

CHAPTER THREE

My Brother, the LARD 'n the Steering Wheel

Once in a lifetime, you get revenge on someone who has caused you grief. Once in a while, the little kid gets the big kid right where she wants him. That day was one of those times.

Just beyond the door of our farmhouse was an old run-down shed where we kept the John Deere tractor. The "Deere" was our newest tractor; it was about 25 years old and Dad's pride and joy. Right outside the shed were a dying cherry tree and my swing set.

One afternoon, as I hung from the top bar of the swing set, minding my own business, my brother called to me from the tractor shed.

"Dor-is, come he-re!"

Now, we'd been at each other's throats all day. Mom had said he was not to talk to me, and I was to leave him alone, too. So I reminded him.

"Mom said I don't have to, s-o ther-re."

"Why don't you go 'n get Mom?"

"You can't make me. Na na na na na na."

"Better co-me in here or I am going to pound y-ou," Mark called.

Well, enough was enough! I ran into the house to get my mama and the broom. I wanted Mom to smack Mark with the broom and make him quit talking to me.

Of course, as soon as I'd picked up my weapon of choice, Mom wanted to know what I was up to. I told her Mark was being a poop and that we needed to get the broom and get whacking if we wanted him to shape up. She decided she'd tag along and see what was going on.

Once back in the shed, we found out what had started the conversation. Mark was there on the seat of the John Deere with his head poked thorough the spokes of the steering wheel! Apparently he had put his head in there so he could see the gauges. When he tried to pull it back out, he found out he was stuck! He had been working on getting his head out of the steering wheel for a long while and all that pulling and pushing had made his ears swell up.

That was great news for his little sister!

My mother was able to show genuine concern for my brother. She tried to help him get his head out. She tried twisting him different ways, getting one ear out first. She tried to take the steering wheel off the tractor. Nothing worked.

Mark was starting to panic. He started screaming bloody murder, and his arms and legs flopped around like a chicken with its head cut off. Finally, as a last resort, Mom sent me back in the house to get a crock of lard.

Now, the lard at our house wasn't that fancy white stuff you buy at the grocery store. We had real lard, from a real pig we'd really butchered in the machine shed a few weeks before. It smelled bad and had little chunks of stuff in it. It was nasty. I was happy to get it for my big brother. Out of the house I came with a big, nasty crock of old yeller lard. I'd looked over my choices and picked out the worst looking mess I could find. I held it at arm's length all the way up from the basement and out to the shed.

Mom stuck her arm in the crock, scooped up a big bunch of slime and began to rub it all over Mark's head. He kept squealing and screaming and flopping around. I decided to help too. I spread lard all over his face, in his nose and every once in a while, a bit went into his mouth as well, until Mom said I couldn't help anymore.

Mark's head still would not clear the opening in the steering wheel. Eventually Mom decided we needed to get his body even with the steering wheel so it would be a straight shot pulling him out. We piled boards over the seat until he was lying flat on his back, his head even with the steering wheel. Mom was not about to give up; she pushed each of his ears backwards up against his head, tied a string around to hold 'em there and greased him up like a pig again. She told him to hold still and quit squirming around 'til she got him loose. Bound and determined to free her screeching child from the clutches of the cold machine, she climbed up on the metal plate at the back of the tractor and pulled for all she was worth. There was a loud sucking sound, followed by a scream and a POP! Out he came!

By the time we got him out of there, his ears were red as fire! He was covered with goop from head to chest and smelled kinda rancid. Things were starting to get back to normal. Soon as he was freed, I took off for the house. I was pretty sure he'd want to thank me in a special way for stuffing the lard up his nose.

Later that evening, Mark was nicer to me than he ever had been before—or since. He promised me everything but the moon if I swore never to tell anybody about the lard and the steering wheel.

He never said I couldn't write it down.

CHAPTER FOUR

SINK OR SWIM

Binder Twine 'n Bandaids

Sharon, who's ten years older than me, was the oldest kid left at home, at least for a while. Sharon has lots of good points, but one thing about Sharon, you can't let her get near any water. Sharon sinks, big time. She never learned to swim a lick. We didn't even let her fill the bathtub all the way to the top. When she was a kid, every time she got near water, her arms and legs would start flailing about, and somehow she managed to get her head to go under. Sooner or later, someone had to go and get her. It happened every time. We knew this about Sharon.

One summer, on one of our annual treks to the West, we ended up at the Pacific Ocean. Since we all knew that Sharon and water didn't mix, she had orders to stay up close to the shore and not to get into any water over her ankles.

The rest of us have some swimming ability, all rated by our ability to retrieve Sharon when the need arises. I can swim well enough to get myself out of trouble, but I wasn't strong enough to go in the deep water after Sharon. Dad could get her out, but he didn't particularly like to swim; he liked to fish. So he usually wasn't dressed for the part when it came time to go in and get Sharon. Mom liked to float on her back, but if all else failed, she'd get Sharon and drag her kicking and screaming out of the water. Mark was a strong swimmer, with broad shoulders and a tiny waist. He was fast and good at the rescue roundup. Mark was usually the one to get Sharon out her perils. It was a little tricky; he was smaller than she was, and she could really put up a stink when she was going under for the second or third time. But, experience is a big factor, and Mark learned to come up underneath her and shove her up on shore before she got a good hold on him. We all knew our place, we all knew what to do when Sharon got in too deep, and we all knew it wouldn't be long before she was flapping around again, needing help. Like a moth drawn to a light in the darkness, Sharon was drawn to deep water. She couldn't help it.

Dad tried to teach Sharon to swim as a safety precaution, but he hadn't had much luck. Mom paid for her to take swimming lessons in town at the YMCA. During the final lesson when all the kids had to swim across the big pool, Sharon jumped in and stood at the bottom. No kidding. She could actually stand at the bottom of the pool. I tried to do that, and I kept coming up to the top, but Sharon could do it easy. Everyone watched and waited for her to come up. But there she stood, air bubbles coming out of her nose, just waiting at the bottom of the pool to die. Finally the instructors jumped in and dragged her out, and she started coughing and choking up water. Sharon was never going to learn to swim. We needed to keep her away from any water deep enough to cover her feet.

So there we were at the ocean, in a deserted little place along the highway. I was swimming out and letting the waves bring me back in. Dad was sitting on the shore being the lifeguard, Mom was floating along on her back watching the clouds, and Mark was way out on the horizon. Sharon was sitting in the water up close to the shore, squealing any time it covered her knees. She was wearing one of Dad's long-sleeved shirts and had the tails tied around her waist. Not only did she try to drown when she got next to water, but she burned, too. Sharon was a misfit. But Mom 'n Dad told us we had to keep her, so each time I got close to the shore, I checked to make sure her feet were still in the water and her head was above the waves.

We'd been playing there about an hour when a wave washed me up on shore and I noticed that Sharon had left the safety of the sandy shore and was now walking on rocks over in a little cove next to a tiny cliff. It looked safe enough to me. How deep could the water be around those rocks, anyway? I looked around for Dad, and I could see him over by the truck, not far from her, checking out his fishing gear. I swam out for another turn at body surfing.

Once I got out in the ocean a little ways, I heard the familiar racket of Sharon flopping around. Since it was everyone's job to keep her head above water, those of us in the water started swimming toward the sound. I stopped for a moment to call out to Dad that Sharon was in over her head again, and he started to run toward her.

Mark was coming, but he was a long way out there, and Sharon had apparently slipped into a pool of water deeper than I was allowed to swim in. She was screaming and taking on water. Her arms and legs were waving like a flag loose in the breeze. The shirt had come untied and was covering her face. Every once in a while, her head went down and her feet stuck out of the water like a duck searching for food at the bottom of a lake. Mom yelled at her to close her mouth and hold her breath.

Mark passed me up and he was really moving. He cut through the water like a shark after its prey. Sharon was still screaming, and I don't think she heard Mom's directions. Dad ran through the sand, stripping as he came. He was down to his swim trunks and his black shoes. He hopped on one foot, trying to get the last shoe off. He reached the edge of the rocks just as Mark grabbed on to Sharon's waist and gave her a heave. He threw her about twenty feet closer to the shore. Her arms and legs were still flailing back and forth during the flight. She was close enough to shore at that point that if she would have just stood up, the water would have been about waist deep. Sharon was too scared to stand up. Her arms were still flapping and her feet kept coming to the top. Mark headed for her again; he was going to give her another shove. I started swimming toward her, too, thinking I might get to be the one that saved her this time.

Dad stopped running and yelled for her to stand up!

"Sharon! Just stand up!"

We all screamed at the top of our lungs, "Stand up, Sharon!"

Nothing. Sharon couldn't hear us. It must have been that shirt over her head blocking her ears.

Mark reached her again He stood up and was going to grab her arm and help her get her feet on the ground. She took one look at him and tried to crawl up his back and get on his shoulders. Mark was smaller than Sharon and tired from his rapid trip in from the great beyond. He wriggled loose and started heading out to deep water again. Sharon was not about to let him get away. Somehow she got her feet up on his shoulders and mashed him down to the bottom of the ocean. Then, while she was standing on top of his back, she continued to scream for help.

I was close enough now to reach out and touch Sharon, but I wasn't sure what to do. Sure, she had tried to drown Mark lots of times before, but never in this particular fashion. I didn't know whether to try and push her off Mark, or help her back to the shallows. I turned around and called out to Mom to ask what she wanted me to do about Sharon.

Sharon heard my voice, turned and tried to get a good grip on me! Arms and legs were flying everywhere, and with a grip like a vice, she reached out and grabbed me by my hair. She pulled me over backwards, started clawing at my face and shoved me under the water. I came up for air, got a full breath and started swimming for the shore under the water so she couldn't see me and get hold of me again. Every man for himself, I thought.

By then, Dad had taken the plunge, but he was still far away from us. Mark had thrown Sharon to the other side of this little pond, and Dad had to get all the way across the rocks to reach water deep enough for him to swim. Mom came to the forefront. She suddenly realized that not only was Sharon going to drown, but apparently, she was planning to take the other two kids down with her.

Mom got up close to Sharon and grabbed her by the shoulders to try and talk some sense into her. Sharon was way past that, so Mom did the only thing left—she doubled up her fist and belted Sharon right in the face. Sharon stopped drowning, stopped screaming and stopped wailing.

Then she started to cry. Mom grabbed her by her shirt and dragged her up to the shore. I went back to check on Mark. As soon as Mom pulled Sharon off his back, he came up for air. He looked a little beat up and his face was a funny gray color, but he was still breathing. I got a big scratch along my cheek and down my neck and was missing a big hunk of hair. Mom's knuckles were swollen, Sharon was gasping for air, and Dad was trying to figure out what happened to his glasses.

We each started walking back through the sand, picking up the clothes strewn along the path as we went. Sharon was still bellyaching about her swollen nose. Dad was really crabby about his missing glasses. Mark was too tired to say anything. Mom warned Sharon about the dangers of getting in too deep, and I was just thankful to be alive.

It had been pretty much a normal summer day. Whenever we let Sharon get close to the water; we knew what we were to expect, and Sharon always lived up to our expectations.

CHAPTER FIVE

Playin' "CRO-GOLF"

The family that plays together stays together, unless it is a big brother and a little sister. In our case, the family that played together…tore up the front yard.

It all started when my folks got called down to southern Illinois to help out my grandparents, about a year after we'd moved out to the farm. It was the one and only time both parents went away and left me in the care of my older brother.

Now, my folks had worked very hard to get our front yard looking decent. The rest of the place was still a junkyard, but the front yard looked very nice.

Just before they left, they had taken out an old plum tree from the edge of the yard and left a little hole there where the stump had been. Dad said he was going to fill it in as soon as they got back home.

Mark and I were playing croquet when they drove off down the driveway. We were trying to convince our folks we could stay on the farm alone for two days without killing one another.

Just as the truck went up over the hill, Mark hit his ball and it rolled into the hole left by the plum tree. "Hey, this is like golf, only with croquet balls! This might be a new game! 'Cro-golf'!" Mark was excited, and it showed in his voice.

We knew that real golf courses have 18 holes; we only had one. We would have to do something about that! After much discussion and planning, we determined we needed 17 more cro-golf holes. Mark knew how to use a post-hole digger, so we got right to work. We drew up our plan on the back of an envelope and started digging. We took the dirt from the holes and made little volcano-looking piles to make the course challenging. After several hours of concentrated effort, Mark and I'd built the world's first full-service cro-golf course, right there in our front yard.

We had all kinds of obstacles on our golf course. We brought in drainpipes to hit the ball through. We had boards you had to use to tee off. We created brick obstacle courses for the balls to go around. We had little fences you had to maneuver past. We brought all kinds of junk up from the gully and strategically placed choice pieces throughout the cro-golf course to give it style.

Then we decided we needed a sand trap, so out to the barn lot we went to get a few wheelbarrows full of sand. Pretty soon, we'd made the most fantastic sand trap, right in the middle of the course. We played cro-golf and enjoyed twenty-four hours of peaceful bliss.

When night fell, Mark found a treble light and ran a drop-cord from the house out to the big oak tree so we wouldn't have to stop playing. Treble lights are the best invention in the world, a big, long drop cord with a huge, bright light bulb hanging on the end. How great is that? The only thing better than a drop-cord is a treble light. There hadn't been any time to put away our tools, so we propped the posthole digger up against the wheelbarrow on the front porch.

Apparently Mom 'n Dad had tried to call home and check on us a few times, but we were outside day 'n night playing this new wonderful game. They got worried when no one answered the telephone and decided to come home early.

They pulled up in front of the house about midnight. Dad got out of the truck and stepped in the first cro-golf hole.

"We must have moles! Look at all these holes in the front yard!" he told our mother in a loud voice.

As soon as Mark and I heard the yelling and swearing coming from the driveway, we each sat bolt upright in our beds. Oh boy, trouble was brewing. We scrambled down the stairs and stood in front of the wheelbarrow and post-hole digger, trying to look innocent. We acted totally surprised to see all the holes, and we wandered around behind Dad, inspecting each one, just like we'd never seen them before in our lives.

Dad kept remarking on the way these holes looked. He turned on the headlights so he could get a better view. Dad wanted a flashlight!

Our dad was a smart guy. It only took him a few minutes to put the puzzle pieces together. Sand traps, obstacles all over the yard, two croquet mallets and two croquet balls, a post-hole digger and a wheelbarrow... Hmmmm, something was fishy here.

He looked both of us square in the eye and said, "Which one of you wants to be the one to tell me what happened to my front yard?"

Well, that was a loaded question for the younger of the two offenders. I could rat out Mark and send him up the river, but it would only be a matter of time before I'd have to face the penalty he'd charge to my account. I could lie to Mom 'n Dad, knowing full well they had already figured it out. Or I could just stand there in my PJs, looking stupid. I chose the last option.

Eventually Mark opened his mouth to speak. I guess he figured with the post-hole digger right there and everything, it would be better to come clean. I just held my tongue and let him take the rap.

The next morning I got up, ready to pay the price for tearing up the front yard. To my surprise, I found Mark and Dad digging post-holes in the gully next to the house. We played cro-golf out there for the rest of that summer and part of the next. The thing about playing in the gully was that we didn't have a drop-cord that could reach that far, so come evening, you had to call the game. And in some peculiar way, it was never as much fun as it was that first night, with the treble light swaying from the tree branches, the cool breeze blowing in from the hillside, and me 'n Mark laughing and trying to see who could make the most unbelievable shot, right out there in the front yard.

CHAPTER SIX

the Tractor INCIDENT

Our first year on the farm, we had a very wet spring. Dad was behind in his planting schedule and needed lots of help. One day, before heading into town to his "paying job" at the International Harvester plant, Dad told my brother that he had to plow the remaining eighteen acres before he could go on his date, and Mark was trying to get finished before evening set in.

About an hour into the job, Mark got the "Deere," our big green tractor, stuck in the mud at the end of the field. He walked up to the house and I was the only one home. Mom had run off to town to pick up some groceries, and left me in charge of the house.

"I need another tractor to pull me out of the mud. Can you drive the 'M'?" The "M" was our big red International Harvester tractor.

"Sure," I said. "You'll have to start it for me, and I'll bring it down to you." I was eight years old. What eight-year-old would say no? The plan sounded good to me as I said it. I knew I wasn't strong enough to turn the crank to start the engine, but I was pretty sure I could drive it once he got it going.

Sure enough, Mark started up the red monster, and I saw him walking toward the barn where we kept the log chains. I climbed up on the seat and looked over my options. There was a long handle to my right, and the lever thing on top that made the tractor sound louder. I opened the throttle all the way up and little flames shot out of the top of the pipe. I'd seen Mark do it lotsa times! Next I reached down and pushed the tall red handle forward, engaging the clutch. The tractor had been left in first gear, and it heaved forward and started picking up speed. I grabbed onto the steering wheel with all the strength I could muster, and drove the tractor straight though the side of the barn!

The rear wheel caught the corner post of the building, and the roof started to fall in. I swerved right and just missed Bossy, our milk cow. There were two big bumps that slowed me down when I ran over the sheep. Totally out of control, I headed toward the orchard, catching a fence post between the rear axles as I went. The tractor pulled the fence line out all the way along the barn lot! Then, with the fence still dragging behind, I yanked the steering wheel hard to the right. The tractor tipped at an angle, hit the ditch, fell on its side and died. I jumped off. Mark turned and faced the mess. His mouth moved but no sound came out.

Mark came a-running over and as soon as he got up to where I was standing, we heard Dad's truck coming down the lane. My big brother and I stood there in silence, the epitome of shock and awe. Neither of us moved.

Dad drove by the "M" lying on its side and slowed down. As he followed the lane and saw the fence and posts piled in a tangled heap, the truck slowed to a crawl. He passed the two sheep carcasses in the barn lot, but he kept on coming. By then, cattle, sheep and horses were wandering along the side of the lane. When Dad crested the hill and saw the roof sagging over the big part of the barn, well… he just stopped the truck right there in the middle of the road.

Dad got out, left the driver-side door hanging open, took off his cap, rubbed his forehead, surveyed the damage, and with a weak, unsteady voice croaked, "What in the heck happened here?"

I couldn't think of a lie, so I said, "Daddy, I drove your tractor straight though the side of the barn, killed them two sheep, pulled out that fence row, 'n now the tractor is layin' over there in the ditch!"

Dad shook his head, lowered his shoulders and said, "No sh--?"

Like any good daughter, I answered his question.

"No sh--, Daddy!"

That was the first time in my life I'd ever so much as uttered a swear word. For two weeks afterwards, I lay awake at night, afraid he was going to beat me for cussing!

The next morning, I woke up while it was still dark and I could hear my Mom 'n Dad talking about the calamity. I couldn't make out all the words they were using; "lucky" was in there, along with "stupid," "rebuild," and a few words I can't repeat here. They were also thinking of selling some sheep.

Now that I am grown and have a better understanding of what they were talking about—luckily no one got hurt. Stupid thing for Mark to do. They'd have to do something with the animals until they could rebuild the barn and the fence. Probably need to sell some sheep to make up for the financial loss. Maybe the tractor was out of commission for a while. I bet they kept coming back to the "lucky" part.

Forty years have come and gone, and Dad has never

mentioned the incident to me again. Even today, if you go out to the "old place," you can still see the evidence of my actions. When they fixed the barn, they left off the part I tore down. The fence was put in a different place. They made the garden into a pen for the animals, and the pen still remains. The mighty "M" still stands in its rightful place next to the corncrib; once they got it out of the ditch, I don't remember it every being moved again.

I think about that day often. The what-if's make my blood run cold. Sometimes I watch my mother's face when I'm telling this story, she gets a little teary-eyed and it always seems like her heart skips a beat.

Over time I have learned that luck is not all it's cracked up to be. You can't depend on it in times of serious trouble, and you never know whose side it might be on. Nope, luck wasn't what saved me that faithful afternoon. It was God. God showed up in all His glory and saved me from myself. His timing was perfect, and my whole family was sure glad He showed up when He did. I was the most grateful of all, and surprised, really. I didn't think God knew anything about me at all, come to find out, He'd been watching out for me all along.

CHAPTER SEVEN

My First JOB

Do you remember your first job? Mine started out okay, but then turned sour on me. The first time I remember having a job was just before I turned nine, which was when Mark decided to move to Minnesota, leaving my parents and me to run the show. My folks were older and I was the last of the brood left at home.

On summer mornings, I'd get up to find my mother in the kitchen cleaning and cooking. Usually, Dad would already be out in the barn or one of the fields. He seemed to have a lot to do out in the barns—fixing old machinery or cleaning out a tool shed or repairing the barns themselves.

Most mornings I'd hang around the house until 7 or 8 o'clock, and then my mother would ask me *The Question*.

"What's your Dad doing?"

"I don't know. He's out in the barn, I guess." I always had the same response. It was a good guess and I was usually right. I had a fifty-fifty shot of hitting the nail on the head.

"I'll give you a quarter to go out and watch him," and with that, she'd deposit a glistening quarter in my hand and out to the barn I'd go.

Now, I thought this was a real job. I thought I was out there to watch over my Dad. I was getting paid, wasn't I? I'd squat down near whatever machine he was working on and hand him tools and listen to him whistle or hum a silly song.

After I'd watched him for a bit, he'd walk over and dump a coffee can full of nuts, bolts and washers onto a board and tell me to sort them out. I can still smell that coffee, metal, dust 'n rust mixture whenever I think of the coffee can job.

I'd spend a couple of hours sorting long bolts from short bolts, big washers from the ones with the tiny holes in the middle, and then I'd pick out the nuts and put them in piles by sizes.

When I was all done, my Dad would announce I'd done a fine job. Then he'd give me a quarter and tell me to go in and watch my mother. I didn't know it, but once I was out of sight, he'd gather up all my work and put it back in the coffee can.

Back to the house I'd go, announcing to my mother that Dad told me to come in and watch her for a while. This declaration was always met with a sigh and a glance at the clock. Then she'd get out a button tin and have me sit down at the table and sort buttons.

I loved the button job. So many of the buttons were very fancy, or had ornate decorations surrounding them. I knew each one by heart. I even liked the tin they came in. It was painted blue and had a "pillow-top" lid with needles and pins stuck in the stuffing. You had to be careful around the lid or you could get hurt. It was a dangerous job for a kid, but I could handle it.

Again, I'd do my job dutifully until completion, at which point I was told I did a great job, and now it was time to go out and watch my dad.

If I asked to go play somewhere, take a walk in the woods or go ride my bike, I was immediately relieved of my duties and allowed to go wherever I'd suggested. If I was whiney and wanted to hang around my folks, I had to sort buttons or nuts 'n bolts.

One day, I was sorting nuts 'n bolts when my sister, Becky, and her family showed up. Her husband came out to the barn and asked what I was up to.

"I'm sortin' out these nuts 'n bolts for Daddy," I told him, putting the last nuts into the pile.

"Isn't that the same can you were sortin' out last time we were here?" he asked.

I was shocked. I could not believe it! It was the same can! How many times had I done the same job over and over? I felt like a fool! I took out for the house without even collecting my pay.

Later, after everyone had gone home and I was lying upstairs in my bedroom looking at my jar of change, I started thinking about my jobs. Hmmmm, who was really the dummy? They were the ones paying me over and over to do the same old thing.

It wasn't until I found myself in their same situation that I understood. I am now in my forties with a six-year-old daughter, and I get it. They were just trying to buy some quiet time. How lucky they were to get it for a quarter.

They say you never really know someone until you walk around in their shoes. My folks' shoes will be hard to fill, but I still like to try them on and walk around once in a while. Guess I'll grow into them sooner or later.

CHAPTER EIGHT

School DAZE

I've heard tell that some of the older folks in my family went to one-room schoolhouses. Well, our school was a little more modern than that. We had three rooms, a bathroom and a cloakroom. Out in front of the steps by the main door was a big bar a few inches up from the ground where you could scrape the mud off your shoes before you came inside. Throughout the building were hardwood floors, and you could hear teachers coming, "click, clack, click, clack," long before they reached the door to your classroom.

There were three teachers in the building. None of them were overweight, but all of them were solid. Each one wore pretty much the same thing—black lace-up shoes with a little heel in the back, nicely starched, flower-print cotton dresses, and utilitarian wire-rimmed glasses. Their hair was always neatly combed and put up in tight little spit curls.

Mrs. Bader, the first and second grade teacher, had dark hair and was the loudest. Mrs. Alfred taught third and fourth grade. She had silvery-white hair, was the tallest of the bunch and even though she was the toughest she was my favorite. Mrs. Swift was the smallest and easiest to manipulate. She fluttered around like a hummingbird from one place to another, and was in charge of the fifth and sixth grade class.

Each and every morning, we students had to stand up next to our desks and open up the lids so the teachers could walk by to make sure they were neat and tidy. During the inspection, the littlest to the biggest kid in the building recited the Pledge of Allegiance, the Preamble to the U.S.

Constitution, and the Gettysburg Address. If you decided to mumble your words, you got to say the whole thing over again by yourself, up in the front of the room, where everybody could see you.

Our school had its own rules. Everyone followed them or else! All the girls wore dresses, all the boys wore slacks. No blue jeans were allowed. If you planned to play on the monkey bars, you could wear shorts under your dress, but you had to take them off after recess. No spitting, no swearing, no running in the building, no fighting, no crying, no whining, were part of the rules, too. Everyone knew the rules, and when someone broke one, we all waited to see what would happen next. Because something *would* happen! The school practiced swift and consistent justice for all.

I never saw a janitor or groundskeeper or principal. No one of higher authority ever came by. It was obvious to every student in the building that these three women were in charge and could handle anything that came up, and they did.

If you broke a small rule, like your homework wasn't done on time, or you were caught chewing gum in class, or you talked out of turn, you had to go to the cloak room and sit on a chair away from the respectable students.

If you were judged to have participated in a major infraction, such as a fight or letting a swear word slip out on the playground, you were taken down a winding set of stairs into a dark, stinky dungeon called the boiler room to set it out and think about your behavior.

These teachers hit, too. If you mouthed back, one of them would smack you on the back of the head. If you started making fun of other kids, you would be grabbed by your collar and be dragged off for a good talking to. We were never allowed to hang around the teachers' desks unless we had business there.

Every bit of homework had to be done, and done perfectly. If you handed in work that was sloppy or didn't finish every question, you got to do it again, and again, and again, if necessary.

We all had to bring our own lunches, which we ate right at our desks, all at the same time, every day, teachers too. I think that's why they had to do that "desk inspection" thing every morning, just to make sure nothing was growing there. After lunch, we'd all go outside for recess.

Our school had a playground with a merry-go-round, a few swings, some monkey bars, and the biggest teeter-totters you have ever seen. If one kid got on one end, and four or five jumped on the other end at the same time, you could catapult the single rider about 20 feet.

When I was in fourth grade, someone came out in the summertime and built "the blacktop." That was a big improvement to the dusty yard we played on. On odd-numbered days, the boys could use it to play basketball, and on even-numbered days, the girls could use it for hopscotch and to roller skate. Boys didn't roller skate, and girls didn't play basketball. I think that was in the rules somewhere.

Everyone knew who the smart kids were; we all recognized the rich ones, too. We were well aware of where we fit in the order of things. I started out with a few handicaps. I was an "import" and they were "natives." No matter how long you lived there, you could never become a native. To add insult to injury, not only was I an import, but I was one of the farm kids, not a town kid. Everyone knew *which* farm I was from, too, and that didn't help things either. Plus, I was left-handed, which put a major black mark on my portfolio as well. Deep down, I still think that had something to do with my placement in the pecking order in life.

So there I was, the scrawny, left-handed import from *that* farm, with dirty knees and the beat-up, orphan-looking face and tangled hair. Not much hope for me.

Frankie Flowers, a kid in my grade, took it upon himself to remind me every day about my station in life. He loved teasing me and making me cry. Then I would get into trouble, because "no crying" was one of the rules at the school. Sometimes he'd pull on my coat and a button would pop off, or he'd tear the sleeve of my dress by yanking on it too hard. I'd go home and tell my mom on Frankie Flowers! Mom always said she was too big to go up to that school and beat up Frankie, so I needed to handle it myself.

So one day, I stood next to the bar in the front of the school, scraping the mud off my shoes (otherwise it would dry and then make this big mess under my desk when it fell off on its own). I was always embarrassed about the mud on my shoes, but there was no way to keep from getting muddy walking up that dirt road after a rainstorm to wait for the bus.

Anyway, I'd just finished cleaning off my shoes. When I turned around, I found myself standing nose to nose with Frankie. He reached forward and gave me a good shove, and I fell backwards over the shoe scraper. All the other kids laughed. I started to cry and then something inside me just snapped. I got up, wiped the tears off my face, doubled up my fist, and whapped Frankie on top of his head. That stopped the laughter, and a cheer began to grow from the crowd—"Fight, fight! Frankie 'n Dori are havin' a fight!" Most of the cheering was for Frankie's side; he was a native and I think he was right-handed, too.

The cheers seemed to make that flame in my chest grow into a full-fledged fire. Frankie started to back up and I took off after him. I chased him around the schoolhouse and caught him once. We had a big scuffle there, hitting and screaming and slapping and spitting. Then he got away. Mrs. Alfred was outside by then and yelled at us to knock it off and come over where she was. She reached out to grab Frankie, but he ducked and got away from her. *Frankie was always getting away with everything.* I kept up after him. I caught him again down at the stop sign. I beat him up good that time, 'til he got loose again. I chased him all the way back to his house. Each time he'd stop to catch his breath, I'd grab him and smack him around a little more. He could outrun me in the short haul, but I had endurance.

Frankie lived a good six blocks from the school, and I caught up with him at least four times before he hit his front door running at full speed and disappeared from my sight. I wasn't allowed to go into other people's houses, so I didn't follow him in.

So I stood out there in front of his house, yelling, "Come on out, you big, fat chicken!" at the top of my lungs. I made some "buck-buck-buck" sounds like a big old chicken so he'd get my point. I could see him looking out at me from behind the curtains, crying like a baby. I was still mad, ready to go at it all over again!

Finally his mother came to the door and said I should go on home. I hadn't thought of that. I started walking toward the farm. On the way, I figured I'd better clean myself up and refine my story about how Frankie had started the whole thing. Otherwise I was really going to get it when my mom found out I'd been in a fight. So as I walked, I buttoned up my dress with the buttons that were still left. One sleeve was torn and hanging down, so I decided it would look better if I just pulled it all the way off. I pulled up my socks and folded them over real neat. Then I spit on my hands and tried to clean off my face.

Pretty soon, I was at the corner where the blacktop met our lane. I took a deep breath and turned down the road. My steps slowed as I got closer to the house. I could see my mom and my dad sitting out in the yard waiting for me. I decided they'd have more sympathy for me if I developed a limp, so just as I was getting up to the house, I started dragging one leg.

I was coming up on the driveway when Mom spoke up. "I hear you settled your problems with Frankie Flowers this mornin'." She was matter-of-fact, no waver in her voice.

Dad just sat there with a coffee cup in his hand, rocking in his chair. Someone must have called them and ratted me out already. Probably that big baby, Frankie Flowers.

"Yep," I said and kept on limping. I should have won an Oscar for my performance. I winced with every step. Now I had one shoulder sagging, too, and I was doing that whole "right-side-might-be-paralyzed" stagger.

"Better get inside and clean yourself up," Dad said. He was always wanting us to clean up, get over it, and move on. You could come into the house beat up from your daily adventures and unless some part of your body was missing, he didn't want to hear about it. Dad was never good at handing out sympathy; he didn't want to encourage whining.

"Yep," I said. I was up to the sidewalk now.

"Don't s'pose you want to tell us about it?"

"Nope." First of all, I was so mad I couldn't remember half the stuff that happened, and I knew that if I told my folks that Mrs. Alfred had told me to stop and I didn't, I'd get my butt whopped. It was one of those times I figured it would be best to not make eye contact, keep moving, and just try to get to the safety of my room.

I stayed up there a long while, turning the events of the afternoon over and over again in my head. I hid in my room the rest of the day. Mom brought me up a plate for supper and never said a word about Frankie. Dad went on with his work. I went on with my pity party, and Frankie? Well, Frankie Flowers never shoved me down again! In fact, on the days I rode my bike into town, if he saw me, he'd cross the street and walk on the other side.

The weekend came and went, and on Monday morning, when I went into my classroom, all the desks had been rearranged. Frankie was sitting in the very front of the room on the right, and my desk was in the far back of the room on the left. There was that whole left-handed thing rearing its ugly head again.

Somehow, we all survived those early days, a little wiser, a little braver, and a little stronger.

I learned more than spelling words at that old country school. I learned that bullies aren't much to be afraid of once you get your dander up. I learned that everyone cries when they get hurt. I learned it could be good to stick up for yourself and when push comes to shove, you'd best stand your ground and face trouble straight on. As a last resort, you might consider giving it a good bop on the head.

CHAPTER NINE

Brand New MOCCASINS

Vacations. We took a long one every summer, sometimes four weeks in a row. We never had definite plans when we left home; we just had a general idea of the direction we were headed toward. We had no hotel reservations, no list of special places we were going to visit. If we saw a billboard that advertised anything spectacular we would pull off the road and go take a look. Our plans were very flexible.

The night before we started out, I'd sleep in the camper. I wanted to be sure I was already in there, just in case Mom 'n Dad decided to get an early start. We always headed out west, wound our way through mountains and valleys, and eventually made a tour of Texas and then headed back home. We were always ready to get away from the farm, and when the time came, we were always ready to get back to the farm, too.

Anyway, there is one vacation I especially remember. It was the year I got my moccasins. I was ten.

My parents and I left Illinois to go on vacation in the middle of July. We were planning to be gone from the farm for four weeks. We always traveled in a truck with a plywood topper on the back. The topper had a canvas top, so in summer, we used it for a camper, and the rest of the year, when we hauled bales of hay or animals to the auction barn, we had a wooden rack to replace our camper. The old truck was a real all-purpose-vehicle, and we didn't need an inscription on the side to know it.

Mom 'n Dad rode in the front of the old red truck, and I had the back all to myself. There was a cooler back there, full of Pepsi, and the big mattress off Mom 'n Dad's bed. We had propped it up on a piece of plywood over the wheel wells. I slept on it during the day, my folks slept there at night. That year I rode over 5,000 miles in the back of that truck in the heat of the summer. We started out working our way north and west, then down the Pacific coast, back through Nevada and the incident I need to tell you about occurred toward the end of our trip, just inside the Arizona border.

The best thing about that vacation was that we got to eat at restaurants. We would eat breakfast at our campsite; lunch out of the cooler along a stream somewhere, and by early evening, would be looking for the next place to camp. We'd watch for signs or find a place on the map that looked good, and then Dad would announce we should find a place to chow down before setting up camp.

Along the highway, he'd find some little broken-down café, its bright neon lights calling us in off the road. Dad liked to find the ones with lots of semi's in the parking lot. He said it was a good indication of the quality of the food and service.

Dad was a "talker" and he'd strike up conversations with people we'd never met before out in the café parking lots. Sometimes they needed help fixing up beat-up old cars, and my Dad could fix anything. We always carried a toolbox bigger than our cooler filled with tools and spare parts.

Anyway, after we'd pull up in the parking lot, Mom 'n Dad would open up the back of the camper, and I'd roll out. Usually my hair would be standing straight up on my head, and my clothes would be wrinkled and messy. They'd give me orders to wash off my face, brush my hair and find my shoes. They'd spruce me up right there in the parking lots, right on the tailgate of the truck. This always took a while. Sooner or later, I'd pass inspection and we would head inside.

They didn't have kids menus back then, so I could order anything they offered. I'd glance around at the plates the waitresses were bringing out to other patrons and try to get an idea of what I wanted. Dad always wanted chicken-fried steak or liver and onions. I always sat in the seat right next to him, across the table from my mom.

After the meal, there would be a big discussion about where we were going and what we were going to do the next day. Mom was our navigator, and she'd produce a map and point out all the options of different places we might go to see. It didn't matter much to me. I just like riding along in the back, looking out the window and drinking my Pepsi.

One fateful morning, we'd finished breakfast, broken camp and headed toward the Grand Canyon. This was a place I wanted to see. Mom 'n Dad had made a big deal about it before we left home. It was kind of the "carrot" we'd been heading for all along our summer journey.

When we crossed the Arizona border that morning, Dad honked the horn to get my attention and Mom held a blackboard up against the rear window of the cab telling me it wouldn't be long now. She was smiling and pointing straight down the road ahead of us. I knew this was going to be a day I'd always remember.

By lunchtime, we'd reached the outskirts of the canyon, and stopped by a souvenir shop. That was something we seldom did, and I was excited to get out and rummage through the stuff and see if I could talk my folks out of something good.

As I wandered up and down the aisles of Indian dolls and bumper stickers, nothing really caught my eye until I made my way up to the checkout counter. Right there, behind the girl with the long braids, were the most beautiful moccasins I'd ever laid eyes on. They were tan leather with turquoise beads sewn on the toes. They had fringes around the ankles and zipped up the back. I knew I had to have them. I turned to my father and said, "Daddy, can I please have a pair of the beaded moccasins? Please? Please, Dad? Please, Daddy-O?" Whenever I wanted him to know I meant business, I'd call him "Daddy-O."

Dad gave a quick glance up at the counter, smiled at me, and said, "Sure, little lady, as long as you have the money to pay for them."

With that, a light bulb went on in my head. I mumbled something to the clerk and took off for the truck. I clamored up in the back, moved the toolbox, crawled under the mattress, and produced the longest, dirtiest, nastiest sock you can imagine. I emerged from the truck dragging it on the ground behind me.

Dad had followed me every step of the way, never saying a word. Like a dutiful puppy, he followed me back into the shop and let me order my size moccasins from the shelves. Dad was planning to teach me a lesson in economics.

The clerk helped me try on the moccasins, and after I'd pranced back and forth in front of a mirror she had placed on the floor, she announced they fit me perfectly. She rang up my order and declared that the total came to $73.00. Dad let out a snicker, and I lifted my stretched-out, stinky sock to the top of the counter. I proceeded to dump out $154.00 in small bills and change.

Dad's eyes nearly popped out of his head. "Where in God's green earth did you get that kind of money? You only had $10 when we left Illinois!"

I was shocked at his comments. Surely it had slipped his mind and he just needed me to remind him. "Well Daddy," I said in all innocence, "every time we went to a restaurant, you left the change lying there for me on the table."

I'd picked up the tips from Illinois to Montana, from Seattle to Los Angeles, and all the way back to Arizona. Every evening in every town at every café, we'd stiffed the waitress, and I'd stuffed my sock.

Dad was so dumbfounded he couldn't even swear. He just stood there, staring at the shoebox that was wrapped-up tightly with brown cord.

As I walked out to the truck, proud of my new purchase, I heard him regain his voice and tell Mom we could NEVER go to any of those restaurants again in our lifetimes. And we never did.

I climbed up in the back of the truck, moved the toolbox, crawled under the mattress, and deposited the balance of my treasure sock in its secret hiding place. Happily, I settled down on the mattress, opened a Pepsi and admired my new leather-beaded moccasins with the zippers up the back.

Guess I showed him! Dad he wasn't the only one who could teach lessons in economics!

CHAPTER TEN

Pretty as a PICTURE

I dreaded Picture Day at school. If I told my mom it was coming up, she'd try to fix my hair by giving me a home "poodle perm." Those always made me look worse than usual. If I didn't tell her about Picture Day, I ended up with a photograph of my thick hair standing straight up from my head and bangs so long I was barely able to peek out and see the camera guy. It was always a lose-lose situation.

I already had a history of ugly school pictures. The year I'm going to tell you about was fourth grade. On Thursday, our school sent a note home with all the kids letting the moms know that Picture Day was going to be on Monday. Great! Now my mom had a three-day warning. I knew I was doomed.

That Friday night, the annual ritual began. She washed my hair about six times. Then she rinsed it with vinegar water to give it shine. It gave it a smell too, but she said that would go away. After she was sure I was squeaky clean, she started with the home perm. She rolled, she swore, she took a roller out here and there. She put them back in, then noticed she had a few in sideways and had to fuss over that. Mom wasn't sure if she should use the little pink ones, but that's what she had left, and what-the-heck, it had to look better than the straight old stringy hair I usually had.

After what felt like a hundred hours, she had all of my hair up in rollers, and she began to mix this awful-smelling stuff in a small white plastic bottle. I was starting to think that the vinegar smell wasn't so bad after all. She poured her white concoction all over my head, careful to get every roller soaked clean through. It smelled awful and burned my eyes and my scalp. She insisted that I sit with a towel covering my face so I wouldn't pass out from the fumes. Dad always hid out in the barn for these sessions, so he couldn't help me. The dogs had also fled the scene of the crime. My mother and I waited the allotted time listed on the box. When the buzzer over the stove finally rang, mom would begin to yank the rollers from my hair. Time was a factor and she was racing to get the solution out of my hair before the curls permanently secured themselves to the rollers. Once I'd been rinsed and towel dried I could evaluate the damage. Dead cows smelled better than I did, and I looked like I'd stuck my finger in a light socket.

She got out her sewing scissors and tried to fix the mess. She started in the back and I couldn't see what was happening in that little mirror on the kitchen table. Hair, my hair, covered the kitchen floor. Mom was not so much styling my hair as performing a shrub-pruning operation. She trimmed here and there. When she got mad at one curl in particular, she'd just cut it off. She tried to keep me from looking in the mirror, but eventually I caught a glance and was shocked to see how uneven my bangs were cut. With every attempt to straighten them, they grew shorter and shorter. I started to get the feeling that I'd better declare them perfect or I'd be going to school bald-headed. Mom trimmed a little bit more. Now the back of my hair was short, the sides were long and my bangs had a weird-looking asymmetrical angle to them.

Mom finally announced we were done for the night. I was released from the chair and allowed to go to bed. No one said a word about my hair for the next two days, even though it was stuck to my head and little sprigs of what seemed to be bedsprings protruded in every direction.

That Monday morning, I got up at the crack of dawn. Mom had filled the tub with scalding hot water and had a brush she wanted to use to scrub my knees and elbows. The woman had a plan and she was going to make it work! She scrubbed me from top to bottom, hosed me off and made me wear one of my dad's t-shirts over my dress while I ate breakfast. Mom had picked out a red corduroy jumper and a white blouse with a Peter Pan collar for me to wear. She had even purchased new white leotards and black Mary Jane shoes for this special day. School pictures back then were always black and white, but she said red was my best color, and that the jumper would make me look better.

Once I was dressed, she started fixing my hair. At first, she brushed very gently. As time passed by, she started picking up speed. The more she brushed, the bigger my hair seemed to grow. She got out some hairspray that was more like shellac and started trying to tame my mane. Nothing was working. Finally she disappeared into her room, and after a few minutes of things banging and knocking around, she reappeared with a huge white bow about the size of Texas. She proceeded to pull the two long sides of my hair up on top of my head, and with a flood of bobby pins, she managed to secure the gigantic bow right behind my ears. The bobby pins were so tight I could hardly blink my eyes. The scissors came out again. She brushed 'n snipped, snipped 'n brushed. I was still wearing my dad's t-shirt, because we didn't want all that hair to get on my clothes. One more coat of shellac followed by a huge sneeze and I was ready to go to school.

Because it was Picture Day, I didn't have to walk up the lane to the bus. I got a ride all the way to the front door of the schoolhouse. Just as I opened the truck door to get out, Mom reassured me that this year is going to be different. No beaver teeth pictures, no long bangs this year, no wild hair in this shot! This was going to be the year of a good picture for me! She was sure! She told me I wouldn't believe how different I looked when these pictures came back!

I went on in the school, and the morning class went along fine. Everyone said I looked really nice, and I was enjoying all the attention. Later in the day, when the first recess came, I played a nice quiet game of jacks, so as not to mess up my clothes and hair. By lunchtime, most of us kids had forgotten all about the pictures. It was the girls' turn to use the blacktop and I was out there jumping rope with everybody else. In case you hadn't noticed, I was a little bit of a tomboy, so when I jumped, I REALLY JUMPED! It didn't take much of that to start the fall of the Texas bow. First it started to lean to one side, and then later, it got loose from my head and was only dangling on to the end of one strand of my hair. Finally it fell right off on the ground and got stomped on a few times. Now it was a big, dirty, bent-up bow the size of Texas.

I wasn't used to jumping rope in slick-bottom Mary Janes, so it wasn't long before I slipped and fell on the blacktop, tearing a big hole in the knee of my new white leotards. There was a string hanging down by the hole, so I tried to pull it off, and it went clean around my knee, letting the bottom of the leg of my tights fall down around one ankle. All that jumping and running had made my neck start to sweat, and now those pretty curls had turned into a big ball of twine and we were back to bed springs sticking out of my head. To make matters worse, if that was possible, while I was having my bologna sandwich lunch, a big blop of ketchup fell down the front of my blouse, leaving a stain in the shape of a malnourished goat.

Here came the picture guy.

All the kids lined up in A-B-C order, and I was in my place when one of the teachers walked by and noticed I was in dire need of a make-over.

She and her colleagues shuffled me off to the bathroom, washed my face and tried to get control of the shellacked hair. After several attempts, the teachers formed a huddle and decided that the only thing left to do is to wet it down. They dumped the bow in the trash and produced a brush; they let it soak it in the sink awhile, rallied the forces and began to fight with my hair. They made me take my blouse off and turn it around so the skinny goat stain wouldn't show. They also wanted me to take off my leotards and go without any socks, but I knew better than that! I was NOT gonna be caught wearing my new shoes without any socks. No way, not gonna do it! They couldn't make me!

It was my turn with the camera. I sat on a little stool with my ankles crossed, trying to hide my torn tights. They had me sit at an angle from the camera because they thought it would look best that way. The collar of my blouse was choking me because it was on backwards, and I knew that if I smiled, you would be able see I had some empty spaces where I was waiting for my grown up teeth to come in. My hair was wet and combed straight back, leaving me with a scary, windblown tumbleweed effect, and a big ball of curls sprouted in the middle of my forehead where my bangs used to be. I was ready for my close-up. I squeezed my lips together, determined not to show the spaces of missing teeth, and the flash went off.

There you go! Mom was right again! I had no idea how different I was going to look. When Mom finally got those pictures, I bet she was pretty surprised, too.

CHAPTER ELEVEN

the Popcorn BALLS

When you live on a farm, Trick-Or-Treat takes on a whole new meaning. As soon as fall came around, we would start staking out our Halloween goodie tour. We knew that if we stopped at Andersons', we would get big, thick sugar cookies with sprinkles all over them. We knew that if we drove down to the preacher's place, we would get full-size candy bars, but the real quest involved Bergstrom's, my sister and the popcorn balls.

My sister, Sharon, would drive all the way home from Chicago, just to get those popcorn balls! We are not talking about the scrawny, store-bought, food-colored, artificially flavored things they sell now. Our journey was for Mrs. Bergstrom's special caramel-flavored, hand-packed, jumbo-sized, individually wrapped, buttery-rich and golden brown popcorn balls. They were heavy, good tasting and huge. I think one popcorn ball would feed a family of four for three days!

So, every year, come Halloween night, we would make our run. It didn't matter what day everyone else was trick-or-treating, Mrs. Bergstrom only observed the real day. Bergstroms' was always the last stop, because if you got there late enough, Mrs. Bergstrom would give you all she had left. Not many trick-or-treaters go out to the farms, so she usually had plenty leftover in her big basket.

Maybe you wouldn't think going to a neighboring farm to pick up popcorn balls was a big deal, unless you knew about the geese. All the townspeople knew about the geese, which is another reason Mrs. Bergstrom always had a big bunch of her famous popcorn balls left at the end of the night.

The Bergstroms had more geese than anyone I knew. They must have had a hundred or so, and they were some mighty mean geese! They never had a dog, because those geese were more effective in protecting the farm than any watchdog could ever hope to be. They'd be scattered around the yard, minding their own goose business, looking peaceful as could be. As soon as they heard the car door slam, they'd come running from every direction, surround you, and start biting you on your behind, honking at the top of their lungs, and flapping their big, white wings the whole time.

I was terrified of the Bergstrom geese, so every year, before Halloween, I'd start working on my popcorn ball recipe. I'd make popcorn balls for a solid week before Sharon came home. I'd make regular ones, caramel ones, ones with little bits of marshmallows in them. I'd offer up all my savings to buy her popcorn balls, if only she wouldn't make me go over to Bergstroms' that year.

No matter how hard I tried, Sharon was bent on getting those treats. She could not be dissuaded by store-bought look-alikes. She was not interested in my concoctions, and she was not shy about reminding me she had just driven 200 miles to take me trick-or-treating. We were going to Bergstroms', and that was that. I noticed she always drove, and she always stayed hidden in the car.

The scene was the same every year. It was dark, the front porch light was on, and there we sat in the car in Bergstroms' driveway. I was trying to get up enough guts to run for the door. I made Sharon pull up as close as she could to the house. She backed around and jacked around until the passenger door faced the front porch. She turned off the headlights and we'd sit there, peering through the darkness, trying to get a feel for the "goose situation." No geese. We didn't see a single one. Sharon would try to tell me that they were in a pen somewhere, but I knew better. I'd been down this route before.

Pretty soon, it became obvious that Sharon was not leaving until I got the popcorn balls. I took one more quick glance over the property, opened the door, and bolted for the front porch. I doubled up my fist, banged on the door and screeched out "Trick-Or-Treat!" The whole time, I watched for them. I knew they were coming. From somewhere in the back of the house, I heard Mrs. Bergstrom get up from her chair. She was old and it took her a while to get going. I did some kind of dance and prance routine on her front porch and thought that I should just ask her for the recipe so I wouldn't have to come back here again, ever.

While Mrs. Bergstrom was gathering up the basket of treats, the geese showed up. They came in from every direction—you'd think I was holding a bucket of cracked corn! They honked and flapped as I wildly swung my sack at them. They started tearing at the sack. By then, I was beating on the porch door. It felt like a scene out of a Hitchcock movie. The huge birds backed me up against the door of the porch at the front of the house, and I had nowhere else to go. Pretty soon, the closest one took the first bite. Soon, I was screaming and kicking and waving my arms all around. Sharon turned on the headlights. That was her way of coming to my aid.

After what seemed like hours of pinching, biting, screaming, and flapping, Mrs. Bergstrom slowly opened the screen door. I jumped over the top step onto the front porch. I am panting and sweating. Thank God! I made it!

The old woman fiddled with the clean, striped towel and pulled it off the top of the basket, revealing her treasure. Like she did every year that Sharon and I came out there, Mrs. Bergstrom told me she thought everyone who was going to come had already been by, and that I should take the rest of the treats.

She got me a new paper sack and filled it to the top with her special delicacy. I thanked her and mentioned that she had a lot of geese. I nervously glanced out the screen, and she assured me the geese were just noisy. She went on to tell me the headlights made them jumpy, but that they never bit. I considered showing her my hind side and telling her that every kid in town had been bitten at least once. Mrs. Bergstrom went back in the house and turned off the porch light. I was still standing there, peering out into the darkness through the screens, when Sharon honked the horn. She wanted her popcorn balls.

I rolled down the top of the sack to close it, grabbed it tightly in my left hand, flung open the screen door, and jumped all the way from the top step to the sidewalk. That was a bad idea. When I landed, I must have bent down to get my balance. The geese came from the shadows and swarmed all over me. They bit my ears and my arms, my legs, my butt and my ankles. I stood up and started running for the car. Sharon reached over and opened the passenger door. When the geese started closing in on her, she shut it again.

There I was, beating on the window of the car, surrounded by geese. They were too close for me to open the car door, so I jumped over the trunk and made my way to the other side. I opened the rear door and hopped in. Safe on the back seat, I sat there, catching my breath.

Sharon said I sure took my sweet time getting the job done. She was peeved that she had to wait so long and wanted to know if I had gotten the popcorn balls so we could go home. She kept shouting "Didja get 'em?" and glancing in the rear view mirror to make sure that no geese had gotten in the car with me.

DID I GET 'EM!!! DID I GET 'EM??? What did she think I was doing out there? Yes, I got 'em, and about a hundred bruises left by the geese to prove it! I crawled up over the seat and took my place next to my sister.

"Don't leave 'em in the backseat! We don't want anything to happen to the popcorn balls!" Sharon screamed at me.

I sat there, rubbing my bumps and bruises. Sharon was ticked that I made such a big deal about a few geese, and thought I should "grow up."

I thought so, too. Then I could be the driver and watch Sharon make the popcorn ball run. I'd be willing to bet that after one turn of beating off those geese, she wouldn't be so sure that the store-bought popcorn balls weren't as good. I smiled at the thought of trading places with Sharon, and picked up the first popcorn ball. Whew, another whole year before I'd have to do that again! That gives me 365 days to work on my popcorn ball recipe. I started working on it the first thing in the morning.

CHAPTER TWELVE

the Name GAME

Did you ever know someone, who, no matter how hard they tried, could not pronounce your name? Me, too. It was my dad.

My first name is Doris. Dor-is. Like Doris Day. I was very proud and bragged a lot about being named after Doris Day. She was beautiful, graceful and blonde. She could sing and had a dazzling smile. Our name was the only thing we had in common, but I had hope.

Now back to the part about my Dad.

Dad had a way of waiting 'til I was about halfway between the house and the barn lot, and then letting out this gruff roar from the barnyard he'd say my name. "DORSE!"

From a distance, you would hear my mother shout, "It doesn't rhyme with HORSE!"

This statement would make my dad cock his head as though he were listening for further directions. When none followed, he'd use a different name altogether. Changing his tone to a sing-song kind of voice, he'd belt out; "Dorsey-O".

My mother was not about to give up. "'Dorsey-O' is not her name either!" she'd declare into thin air. I am not sure if she was correcting him, or just making an announcement in general.

Once more, my dad would lift his head, giving the impression that he was not sure if the disembodied voice was his wife's… or God's. He'd glance up at the sky, his eyes darting back and forth, and after deciding he was out of harm's way he'd give it one more try. Louder this time and with more feeling. "Dorse!"

This would cause the screen door from the kitchen to slam, and a skinny woman, wearing a faded cotton dress with her long dark hair pulled back in a bandanna, would manage to stomp through the grass. No kidding. My mother could stomp though the grass and make noise! Fists clenched, jaw set, and eyes looking straight forward, she'd head out to the barn to do some business.

Dad would stand up when he heard the screen door slam. He'd wipe the grease off his hands and onto his white t-shirt, and stick whatever tool he was working with into the back pocket of his jeans. One knee would bend and he'd put his hands on his hips, dig in his heals, lift his chin, and put on his game face. He was ready to take her on.

Somewhere along the lane, she'd pass me by. When she reached the gate, she'd stick one foot on the bottom board and hike her other leg over the top, mumbling something about grown men who can't say a kid's name right. Tromping right up to him, my mother, a head shorter than my dad and half his size, would say in a defiant voice, "Now you say her name right!"

My dad would stare down at her in total silence.

Mom's eyes would narrow, her mouth would clamp shut and she'd point one long, scrawny finger my way, and restate her position with a single shake of her hand. Dad's gaze would scan her face. You could see him pondering his options. On the one hand, he could stick to his guns and tell her he was going to continue to trash my name every time he said it. On the other, he had to sleep with her. "Dor-isssssss," he'd chant through clenched teeth.

Apparently that was all my Mom needed to hear. She'd spin on one heel, usually say something about what time supper would be ready, and with her goal accomplished and a bounce in her step, she'd start back for the house.

Dad would stand there motionless until he heard the screen door slam once more. When he decided the storm had passed, he'd reclaim the tools from his pocket, squat down and go back to work.

As soon I cleared the gate and got within normal voice range, Dad would say in a much quieter tone, "Dorse, hand me that wrench there next to ya, would ya?" Then he'd glance up at me with this twinkle in his eye, that small sly smile, and a wink. Victory was his once again.

CHAPTER THIRTEEN

the Neighbor's Cows are loose in OUR FIELD

Binder Twine 'n Bandaids

My dad hated talking on the telephone. He never answered it, even if he was the only one in the house. He didn't like it, and he wouldn't do it. A man has to take a stand about the things he really believes in, and Dad believed in not talking on the telephone.

One spring day, I got home from school, and as soon as I finished changing into my work clothes, Mom announced that my dad had a phone call. He was down in the long field working, and I needed to go fetch him. It was an important phone call, and I needed to get a move on. I was supposed to tell him that *she* said he *had* to come in and talk on the phone.

I headed down through the garden, passed the well, and veered up to the short cut through the pasture. There on the hillside was old Winnie, the brown horse with no spirit. Winnie was a real deadhead, and would barely lope even on a good day, unless she was headed in the direction of home. Once she determined oats in the barn were in her future, she could run like lightning. Old Winnie was neck-reined, which means that you could pat her on the left or right of her neck to turn her one way or the other. Since she was such a slow poke, I decided to ride her bareback with a halter down to get my dad.

I grabbed onto her mane and slid up on her back. I'd ridden Smokey, the good horse, a million times bareback, but I always used a bit for him; he had lots more spunk. Once I was on board, Winnie dutifully started the trip to the field, and after lots of prodding and banging, she finally broke into a canter. We were making good time now, and I was thinking that picking up Winnie was a good idea. She wasn't such a bad horse after all, and was much easier to catch than Smoke. "Maybe I'll start ridin' her more often," I thought as we loped along.

We crested the hill, I waved to get my dad's attention, we delivered the message, and turned back toward home. Winnie and I plodded along and I headed her toward the creek, trying to take my time to get back up to the house. If I get there too soon, they might have work for me to do. I'd be better off taking my time now. The horse and I turned off the lane and started up between the fields. Suddenly Winnie realized where we were headed — back to the barn! There were oats in the barn! Winnie had a one-track mind.

She broke into a trot, and in no time at all, was loping along the fields. I didn't mind. I was a good rider and had no trouble staying on. She began to snort and flip her tail, and then started a flat-out run for the barn. I was starting to lose my grip so I leaned forward and wrapped her mane around my hand a few times. I dug my knees into her sides and leaned up on her neck to get a better grip. She didn't like me that far up on her neck, so she did a little buck-step that scooted me up even farther. Now I was really having trouble holding on. Winnie did one more mid-air buck and I fell over to the side. I wrapped my arms and legs around her neck and fell all the way around to her chest. We were looking eye to eye, and I was upside down.

Her eyes were open wide, she was snorting, and with every step, was pounding my back with her knees. I screamed "Whoa! Whoa!" at the top of my lungs, bouncing up and down from the neck of this crazy animal. and she was probably thinking that I meant "GO FASTER!" She picked up her pace.

Finally the weight on her neck was too much for her to bear. She folded at the knees, dug her bony legs into my belly and began to use me as a snowplow through the creek bed. She must have been thinking that I was the worst rider she had ever seen. Winnie was tired, scared and wanted to go to the barns. She wanted some oats in the worst way ever! She decided that she wasn't going to push me all the way home, so she let out some kind of hissing snort, jumped over me, gave me one good kick to show me who was boss, and bolted for home.

God, I hated that horse! Why did we even keep her? "If I ever make it back to the barn, I am going to slap her silly! She is never getting another scoop of oats as long as I live! I am NEVER going to ride that stupid horse again! Never!" I muttered out loud as I lay there in the creek bed.

I took stock of my situation. There I was, all rolled up in a little ball. My whole body ached. I thought my back was broken. I was wet and muddy, battered, bruised and bloody. I needed help in a big way.

I crawled up to the crest of the hill and could see my folks sitting out in the metal lawn chairs just off the kitchen. They must be talking about Dad's important phone call. All I needed to do was get their attention. I summoned all the strength I could muster, and belted out a half-crying, half-screaming call for help.

"M-A-O-O-O-O-O-O-M!"

With that, my dad stood up out of his chair and said, "I think Jake's cows are loose out in our field."

"M-A-O-O-O-O-O-O-M!" I tried one more time.

"By Golly, I believe they are! I can hear them, too," Mom replied. "You'd better get them out of there before they flounder!"

"M-A-O-O-O-O-O-O-M!" I was up on one arm now; maybe they'd see my broken body lying there in the alfalfa. "M-A-O-O-O-O-O-O-M!"

"What's that out there on the ground?" Dad was holding his hand up over his eyes to block the sunshine. He squinted, trying to get a better look.

"M-A-O-O-O-O-O-O-M!" By then I was sure they had waited too long, I was a goner. I was positive I wouldn't make it back home. This was it. I was going to die right here on this hill in the hay field. I made one last attempt to cry for help. "M-A-O-O-O-O-O-M-M-Y!"

" 'Mommy??' Why, that must be Doris out there! Doris? Is that you?" my mother cried out.

"Finally, recognition! Help was on the way. The cavalry is coming! I am going to live!" I thought, then collapsed in a heap awaiting my rescue.

Mom headed across the field in her cotton dress and her little canvas shoes. She was wearing her apron, and had a dishtowel in her hand. My mom could fix anything with a dishtowel. She got over to the side of the hill where I lay piled in a heap, ran down a slope and stuck her towel in the creek, then used it to wash off my face. She tied the old wet, sour-smelling thing in a knot around my neck, making a sling for my arm. I had to lean hard on her shoulder as she dragged me back to the house.

Once she inspected me for broken bones and determined that I was just beat up, nothing permanent, she fixed me her cure-all concoction. She sliced onions into a pan, poured some sugar and water over them, added a little drop of camphor oil, and brought them to a simmer. The smell alone could raise a dead man from the grave. She waited until her brew reached the color and consistency of snot. Apparently this stuff would heal wounds, mend broken bones, cure pneumonia, fight off head lice, and dissolve warts. One spoonful would make your nose run, your eyes water and your ears ring. Mom always said it would either kill you or cure you! There were times when I wasn't sure which was about to happen.

She rubbed her goop on my sore spots and had me drink a little of the juice to fight off any infection. She then filled an old bag with ice and had me lie down on the couch to watch TV for the rest of the evening. She even let me eat my supper right there in the living room off a special tray. No chores for me that night!

Good thing, too. I wasn't going to feed that old deadhead Winnie anyway! "I should hobble out to the barn and make her take some of this tonic, that'll show her who's boss around here! Bet she's gonna think twice about banging me up the next time," I thought as I drifted off to sleep there on the couch. Much to my surprise, I lived through the night, and I woke up there the next morning.

CHAPTER FOURTEEN

Combines 'n Bicycles DON'T MIX

Binder Twine 'n Bandaids

I was on my way from the farm to a little town down past the school that day. This town was about five miles beyond the town closest to our farm. One of my teachers lived out that way, and I wanted to see if I could find her place.

It was a wonderful, cool, bright summer morning. I had a three-speed, silver Schwinn bicycle—a hand-me-down from my brother—and I could really get her going when I was out on the open road.

I'd just crossed the town blacktop and was heading west when I saw a man driving a combine just ahead of me. Here was my chance. I stood up and started pumping those pedals like I was riding in the Tour de France. I was picking up speed and gaining on the combine guy.

When I was sure I had enough momentum going, I swung out into the other lane, and passed him, right there on the blacktop! I'd finally gotten up enough speed on my bike to pass something. Yes-sir-ee, Bob, I was somebody now! I was the pass-er, instead of being the pass-ee. I was fast, and I could prove it, I'd passed a guy in a combine! Woo-hoo! I couldn't wait to tell somebody. Yes, sir. I wish I had a banner on my back with my name on it, so that everyone would know that it was me on that bike, passing people on the blacktop!

I glanced back over my shoulder, took one hand off my handlebars, and waved at the guy. I was smiling and laughing! I was a happy kid. He lifted his head in acknowledgement of my effort. He was surprised I was such a fast bike-rider, I could tell. Yep, he'd be down at the tavern tonight, telling everyone about the amazing kid on the silver Schwinn.

About that time, I turned my head to look forward again and there it was—the biggest, deepest pothole you've ever seen. I'm not sure it was really a pothole. It could've been a place where the earth split, and if you fell into it, you would end up in China. This was a crater, a cavern, a sinkhole.

I was going way too fast and I was way too close to miss it. Wham! Bam! Bump! I hit that hole with everything I had, and rode it to the end. My bike did some kind of bizarre contortions in mid-air, and the next thing I knew, I was lying in a pile in the ditch, all tangled up in the mechanics of the bike. One tire was flat, the handlebars were at a strange angle, I'd lost the paper I was taking over to Mrs. Alfred's house, and my glasses were nowhere to be found.

Then along came the guy in the combine. He was laughing and having a good time at my expense. Now he waved at me as he passed me by. He was smiling and nodding, and I was glad his combine didn't have a horn for him to blow.

Yep, he'd be down at the tavern tonight, telling everyone about the crazy kid on the silver Schwinn. I hope he didn't know my name.

CHAPTER FIFTEEN

the Woods on the FARM

The woods were thick out at our place. They were filled with oak, elm and hedge trees, and a few walnut groves. There were blackberries, gooseberries and raspberries that grew wild along the fence lines. Lots of underbrush grew up everywhere, and a small trickling stream meandered through the middle, where narrow paths left by deer and sheep wound their way up the hillsides and back down to the creek bed, through the valley, and finally over to the road.

The bad thing about playing in the woods is that you always had scratches and scrapes on your legs and arms and sometimes on your face. You had that "dirty knees-beat up-orphan" look about you most of your childhood. The good thing about playing out in the woods was that no one ever bothered you, and you didn't have to act like someone you weren't.

Mostly, I liked lying there under the trees when it rained. Unless it was a heavy storm, the rain seldom reached the thick bed of leaves and needles at the foot of the trees. You could hear the raindrops rustle, the thunder would clap, and the lightning would flash, but you never got wet. The trees would bend and sway, then spread their wings to protect you from the storm.

It was peaceful in the woods, but not quiet. Birds and squirrels sounded a warning to everything and everyone that an intruder was among them. Sometimes you would hear a big animal stumbling through the brush, and when it crashed through, you would hope for something exotic, only to find a cow or sheep, or maybe one of the horses.

Rabbits sounded like they were the size of elephants out there in the brush. You seldom saw deer unless you hung around in there until dusk had settled in the valley, and that was getting a little too late for me.

I had an old canvas bag I used to take with me in the mornings; I'd fill it with a book or two, along with green onions, cucumbers and tomatoes from the garden, slices of already-buttered bread, a pocket knife, a salt shaker and a tin cup. You could drink water from the creek, but it always tasted better in a tin cup. You needed the pocketknife to slice up the cucumber and tomatoes. Then you could eat bread-n-butter-n-tomato sandwiches all day. I was set until evening fell, when I'd have to get back up to the house.

No one ever came to look for you, no matter how long you had been gone. Lots of times, I'd wake up early and get going before my folks were up. If they needed you up at the house, they'd honk the horn of the truck, and two long blasts would echo down from the hills. If it was early in the day, the honks meant we probably had company, maybe someone with kids, and they wanted me to come home and entertain. Late afternoon or evening honks meant either a bad storm was headed our way or Mom had a roast ready from the oven. At the sound of the horn, I'd gather up all my belongings and start back toward home.

Once I reached the ripe old age of ten, we had horses on the farm. My favorite horse was Smoke—he was a wild horse who'd come from the mountains of Montana. We'd gotten him for free because no one could break him. They said he was "green broke" when they dumped him off, but what they really meant was that you had to take your life in your hands every time you wanted to go for a ride. Over time, Smoke and I learned to work together. I knew he didn't like saddles, he knew I didn't like getting off the hard way, so I'd ride him bareback down to my special spot in the woods, then let him go on his way.

My special spot was a place where the creek was widest and a big old oak tree stood at the bend (Smoke is buried there now). It was in the center of the woods, and from there you could hear the cars that came down the lane, but they couldn't see you. If you climbed up in the oak tree you could see our eighteen acres, a field at the north corner of the farm. Sitting in that spot, I could hear Dad start his day, and I could tell which field he was headed for from the way the popping of the tractor echoed through the valley.

Once we got to bend in the creek, I'd take off Smoke's bridle and sit and read while he wandered in the area eating grass. He seldom got far from me, but if he got tired and went home, I'd just walk back on my own. Sometimes he'd leave and then later come back for me.

In that special space, I wasn't ugly or lanky. No one cared if I was dirty or my hair wasn't combed. I wasn't judged for my clothes or my grades. I wasn't worried about being popular or rich. The age of our vehicles, or the fact we only had trucks, didn't seem to bother the birds at all, and Smoke took no notice that our house wasn't the one I'd dreamed of having.

Out in the woods I could be who I wished. I could sing loud and off-key. I could yell and holler and make believe anything I dreamed up was true. Out in the woods time was ruled by daylight and darkness. As long as it was light, I'd stay out, but when darkness fell and the last sparkle of sunlight flickered, I'd already be heading through the orchard back to the house.

I knew every path, every thicket, and every hiding place in those woods. If strangers came my way, I could watch them all day without them ever knowing I was near by. Lots of times they came to pick berries or steal apples, and I'd choose my vantage point carefully and study everything about them. I took great pride in knowing they couldn't find me. Sometimes they'd look up, cock their head and seem to stare right at the spot where I hid, almost like they knew someone, from somewhere, was staring back. Eventually, they'd shake it off and go back to their work.

Once I was out there in the middle of a big blackberry patch, picking and eating berries, when a woman came by with a fancy little basket. I watched her climb over the fence and was mesmerized by her attire. There she was, scaling a barbed-wire fence in hose, fancy shoes, a pleated skirt, and a wonderful soft pink sweater. I'd never seen anyone as beautiful as she was out our way before.

I squatted down in the center of the bush, thinking she'd never make it that far. She picked her way carefully through the brush, holding each branch with her pinky sticking out, and slowly made it over to my hiding place.

I watched her for a long while and by the time she had filled her basket, I'd decided she might be someone I'd like to meet, so I jumped up from in the middle of the bush and shouted, "Hey!"

That poor woman started running in place and screaming at the top of her lungs. An instant later, she tossed her fancy berry basket straight up in the air and set a land speed record racing back through the brush and over the fence and into her car. I followed right on her heels, yelling, "Hey! Hey! HEY!"

She was still screaming and crying when she started the car and sped off down the lane.

I walked back and picked up her basket and ate her berries. I couldn't decide if she ran off because I scared her, or because she was caught doing something she shouldn't have been doing. I guess it was a little bit of both.

A little bit later, the horn sounded and I knew it was time to close up shop and head back to the real world. I grabbed my canvas bag and started for the house.

I never told anyone about the "lady" and I never saw her again. But I thought of her often. I remember how wonderful she looked, how much I wanted to be like her at first, and how quickly her tune changed when she realized she was caught while she was up to no good.

I lived my life a little differently after that. I decided people might not be as good as they looked at first glance. I always tried to remember that anywhere, at any moment, someone could pop up out of the bushes and see what I was really up to. I wanted to be sure that if I got caught, at least I'd be caught doing something good.

CHAPTER SIXTEEN

the Bus 'n the BAGGIES

Binder Twine 'n Bandaids

There are days that it just doesn't pay to get up. I've had a few, and I bet you have, too. This is a story of one of those days. Once it started, there was no stopping it. I just had to keep muddling through…

The busses from our school district didn't drive down the lane to pick up the kids. The kids had to walk up the lane and meet the bus. My bus driver was Mrs. Broomfield, and she was always late. For the entire ten years I rode the bus, she was late every single day—except for one—and what a day that turned out to be!

On that day I was in sixth grade, and I was wearing a dress to school because all the girls still had to. It was cold, so I had some big, baggy, red corduroy pants I'd gotten from my cousin on under my dress.

Our lane was a quarter of a mile from the bus stop, and on cold days, I waited at home until the last minute so I wouldn't have to stand out on the corner so long. About half way down the lane was a little hill. You could see the corner as soon as you reached the crest.

That morning, I was taking my time, wandering up the hill, singing my regular songs, when I looked up and saw *the bus*. Mrs. Broomfield had the door open and was honking the horn.

I started to run, legs flying, coat waving in the breeze, lunch box swinging; I was doing what my mother would call "mo-dockin." Anyway, I was running with the wind. I was pickin' 'em up and puttin' 'em down. I thought I was going to make it … until those stupid corduroys fell down around my ankles.

The next thing I knew, I was sprawled out face down in the dirt and had skidded about 300 feet balanced on my nose. My lunch box had sprung open and all my papers and food were scattered out on the ground. My coat and my dress had flown up over my head and when I looked up, everyone on the bus had moved to the windows and was laughing. They were laughing big belly laughs I could hear all the way down the lane.

Mrs. Broomfield finally stopped honking long enough to catch her breath. She was laughing, too. I just lay there, too embarrassed to get up, too winded to ask for help, too sure all 38 kids on that bus had seen my underwear. I reached up with one skinned-up, gravel-covered arm and waved them on.

Mrs. Broomfield hesitated for a minute, and then I heard the screech of the bus door as it closed, and onward went the busload of laughing children.

I remember sitting up and crying for a while. Then I packed up most of the stuff from my lunch box, kicked off the red corduroys and hoofed it the extra mile and a half to school. By the time I got there, I'd missed a good part of class, my skirt was torn, my elbows were bleeding, my lunch wasn't worth eating, I'd lost some of my homework, and my face was red and puffy from outbursts of tears along the way.

Still, walking gave me time to think. I decided that having someone see your underpants wouldn't kill you after all. There is something to be said for a good belly laugh; they say it supposed to make you live longer. Mostly I determined that crying about things doesn't help; it just gets you wet.

CHAPTER SEVENTEEN

just Hangin' AROUND

Our barn had these huge rafters that ran the width of the building. It had two big doors, a little tiny door near the roof, one window, and two big lofts near the ceiling. You could climb up high in the lofts and then jump off the ledge, catch one of the rafters and swing until either your arms got tired, or you lost momentum. Then you'd let go and drop down into the bales of hay far below. It was a great place for a kid to hide out when it was raining, because you could hear the pattering of the drops on the barn's metal roof. There is no other sound like it.

Whenever my Dad would open a bale of hay for the animals, he'd always pull off the binder twine, the string that holds the bale together, and throw it up over one of the rafters so the animals wouldn't get tangled up when they were wandering around the barn lot.

Walking into the barn through the big double doors was always a total sensory experience. On sunny days, the barn seemed dark in comparison to the outside, so it took your eyes a while to adjust when you first arrived. Once inside you could smell the sweet alfalfa bales. If you decided to lie down on the bales of hay, it would scratch and sometimes the rising dust would make you sneeze. Throughout the barn were hundreds of these little loops of twine hanging down from the rafters, like moss on swamp trees.

A rickety old ladder was nailed to the ledge so you could get up to the lofts in the top of the barn if you were courageous enough. The dilapidated old building squeaked and squalled with the wind, and sometimes for no good reason at all, just seemed to heave out a big sigh.

Our hay barn had real personality. I loved it. I spent a lot of time out there sorting out life's problems and acting out books I'd read or TV shows I'd seen. You could yell and holler to your heart's content, and no one would ever hear you. You could see the house from pretty much any vantage point, but there was a gully between the house and the barn that just seemed to suck up all the sound before it reached the homestead. That was great most times, but this particular day, it was not a good thing.

It was a bright fall afternoon, and the winds were picking up, blowing leaves and dust around the yard. As long as you stayed in the sunshine, it was warm enough. If you were stuck in the shade, though, it was cold and the wind cut right through you. I'd been out fooling around in the orchard with the horses, but it was too chilly, so I ducked into the barn for some daydreaming.

Up in the loft, looking over my world, I decided it was time to play an "action game." Action games were different back then. They didn't require a TV or monitor. No Game-Boy, X-box or Nintendo were needed, either. You just cooked up something in your imagination and then played it out right there on stage in front of the sheep and goats or whatever other animal was willing to watch the show. Creating the scenario was far more difficult than chasing a cartoon character around on a screen. You had to stack bales of hay for buildings, prop up pitchforks as people, stick milk buckets on the handles to be the faces. All in all, it took a lot of time and effort just to set up each scene. A good game could take all afternoon.

So there I was, playing my game. I had two mean ol' bucket-head, pitchfork people after me. They had caught me once and tied me up, so I still had some binder twine around one leg. I was planning my getaway, so I rigged up a bunch of binder twine like a grapevine, secured it to the rafter, and I was going to swing from one mountain cliff to the other over an imaginary lake of molten lava. My games were very creative. Our two collies, Ringo and Elsa, were my audience and sat at attention by the doors of the barn, watching my every move.

I grabbed on to my binder twine, let out a bellow and ran like the dickens to the edge of the loft to get up some speed. I jumped high into the air, felt the rope tighten and my arms jerk, and then —something happened. I am not exactly sure of the sequence, but it wasn't good.

When I leapt off the loft, one of my feet must have gotten caught in some of the binder twine on the first rafter. My rope was attached to the middle beam and with all the momentum I'd gathered up from my running start, I ended up twisted and hanging upside down under the loft of the barn with binder twine wrapped around my legs from my knees to my ankles.

I started screaming like a wild man, but no one could hear me. I swayed back and forth from my lofty perch, tangled like a fly in a spider's web, while above and around me, the old barn rafter was heaving and groaning from my weight and the struggle. Both dogs were running in circles, jumping from time to time to see if they could get hold of my shirt, all the while barking to beat the band. I kept thinking that my dad must be around somewhere, and surely he'd hear the ruckus and come save me. Just to test my theory, I stopped screaming and struggling and gave a good listen. Nothing… nada… nobody was coming.

I decided my fate depended on the two collies. After all, they looked just like Lassie. Maybe they'd go for help. "Go get Mom! Get Mom! Go home!" I screamed.

They understood the "home" part. Ringo and Elsa ran from the barn, jumped over the gate, and headed up the lane. I could see them at the front door of the house, barking. "Yes-sir-ee! Whew-Hew! I am going to get some help now!" I thought.

My mom came to the front door, threw it open and both dogs ran into the kitchen to lie down. The screen door banged shut and Mom went back about her business. She didn't even look for me. Big help that was. So much for the Lassie rescue idea. Back to screaming and struggling.

I was exhausted from doing the same thing over and over, and I was getting nowhere fast. I tried to think what some of my heroes would do in this situation. I ran through the Nancy Drew Mystery file in my head…I was able to see the binder twine moss hanging from other rafters and I tried to swing out and grab a few. I imagined that was what Nancy would do—she'd grab onto more twine, get her self upright, untie her ankles and knees, and jump lightly into the hay below, without even getting her pleated shorts dusty. I reached for the closest circle of twine, but as soon as I got a good grip, it fell loose and floated to the barn floor. "Dang it, Nancy gets all the breaks," I thought to myself, frustrated beyond belief. Finally, I decided that I couldn't ever remember reading in any of her books that she had been caught hanging upside down in a barn. It was hard to imagine her blonde hair hanging straight down from her red face. Nancy was not going to help. "I am never going to read another one of her books," I vowed.

Time was moving at a snail's pace. It seemed like I'd been there an hour. All the blood had rushed to my head, the ropes were starting to cut into the backs of my legs, I had a headache, I had to go to the bathroom, and I didn't want to miss supper. This was getting serious!

There is a time in every little kid's life when the rubber meets the road. It's that moment when you know no one is coming to your aid. You have to figure it out yourself. That day in the barn was my time; all I needed was a plan.

It's pretty tough to think of anything after you've been dangling upside down for a while. You can't cry because your nose won't run the right way. I tried screaming again, and that didn't help a bit, so that left the struggling part.

After about fifty tries at grabbing the rafter above me, I figured the twine around my ankles was too long so I needed to shorten the cord, or come up with a "Plan B."

"Plan B" it was. I started to swing back 'n forth, slowly at first, then picking up speed, back 'n forth. I finally got a good rhythm going, back 'n forth. You could hear the barn moaning. Back 'n forth. The twine was starting to unravel. Back 'n forth. I may get out of this alive. Back 'n forth. I'll be home by supper. Back 'n forth. WHOA! Something new! There was a big jerk, the twine was longer. No, wait!

Some of it had broken! One leg was free! Now I was hanging by one leg. “Well,” I thought, “this is an improvement.” Still swinging, back ‘n forth, faster now, back ‘n forth, I’m on a roll, back ‘n forth. Whoa! Another jerk, and my face got closer to the floor.

By now, I was wondering if “Plan B” really was such a good idea. Whoa! Another jerk! The floor moved a little closer yet. It rapidly became plain to me that “Plan B” is named “B” for a reason; I should have stuck with “Plan A,” I’m pretty sure. So, I tried to stop swinging. Do you know how hard it is to stop swinging when you’re hanging by one leg? It’s impossible! I am here to tell you it is impossible to stop swinging and swaying when you are dangling upside down from the loft in a barn by one scrawny leg. It simply cannot be done!

One more jerk, a heave, a sigh, and WHAM! I hit the floor. It was not a graceful, Nancy-Drew type of landing; I made a sound more like when someone throws a bag of feed off a truck. Whump! I hit the ground so hard one of the pitchfork people lost his head, and the bucket cracked me on the shoulder. Then silence.

I lay there a few minutes, trying to decide if I was hurt, and waited for the top of the barn to stop spinning around. There was hay in my shirt, in my hair and up my nose. I had a big old scratch on my leg from something that was under the hay on the floor. There was cow poop on my face, and my arm hurt!

I decided to sit up and try to take stock of the situation. Everything seemed to be working. The barn stopped spinning, and the horse came in and gave me a nudge. Where was he when I needed him?

I could hear the pop of the tractor coming up the lane. It must be time for supper. Dad was never late for supper. The screen door slammed again, and Mom was out in the front yard, calling us in to eat. "Well, better get in there," I told myself. I stood up, brushed myself off, spit on my hand to clean the blood off my leg and headed up to the house.

I was pretty darned proud of myself. Not every kid can fall from a mountain cliff, land in a lake of molten lava, defeat two pitchfork bucket heads, and live to tell about it! Yep, it had been a pretty good day after all.

CHAPTER EIGHTEEN

Wild Cat CANYON

We'd been on the road on vacation a couple of weeks already, and had been camping our usual way. Our truck had been fitted with plywood sides and a canvas roof, and we had an old army pup tent we'd put up to use to store our stuff while we slept. Mom 'n Dad slept in the back of the truck on a full-sized mattress propped up over the wheel wells, and I slept in the cab.

On this particular day, we'd been fishing and fooling around up in the Rocky Mountains. Dad hadn't gotten a single bite on his line and he was feeling pretty low. We needed to find some food on our way to the campground since he had had such a lousy day.

We'd passed a little Mom 'n Pop shop on the way down the mountain, and along with other things, they were selling barbequed chicken and fried taters, Dad's favorite meal. Things were looking up. Dad couldn't resist getting a big bunch. We always had to buy enough food for a small army, so we paid for our banquet and loaded it into the back of the truck. Then we started looking for a place to set up camp. Time was of the essence, since we wanted to get set up before the chicken got cold.

We decided we would take the next available spot, and soon as we saw a sign with that little teepee symbol, we pulled in. It was a sorry-looking campground, totally deserted except for us and a little group of novice Girl Scouts who were trying to get a fire started in a field of dry elephant grass.

My dad was pretty concerned about the prospects of the Girl Scouts getting the job done, and kept saying they might catch that whole place on fire before the night was over. He drove along the winding gravel road until he got to the backside of the park, as far away as he could get from the green-clad goblins and their antics, and backed in between a little cliff and a rocky ledge. I guess he thought we'd be safe from fire there. He walked up the road a piece to be sure we had an exit if we needed it, then came back to enjoy his home-away-from-home cooked meal.

We set all our food out on a picnic table—a big bunch of barbequed chicken and a flat of fried taters. Mom topped our feast off with her standard sliced tomatoes and cottage cheese. We all ate our fill, smacked our lips a few times, then picked up our garbage, put it in a paper sack, and stuck it up on top our camper. Dad said he'd dump it on the way out of the campground in the morning.

We played cards there at the picnic table by the light of a camping lantern and listened to the distant squall of Girl Scout songs until late into the night. We could hear an animal screeching once in awhile, but Dad assured us it was just a big old screech owl and there was no reason to worry about it. We all turned in for the night, Mom 'n Dad in back, me cuddled up in the front of the cab. I had the windows down because it was stuffy up there, and the cool breeze drifting in over my head made the night almost perfect.

A few hours later, I woke up to a loud screech and some growling. I wasn't sure if I was having a dream or if something was up. I sat up and leaned close to the window to peer into the darkness. I couldn't see anything, but the truck was shifting around in the back, so I thought my folks might have heard that noise too. I knocked on the back window and Mom pulled back a curtain and turned on a flashlight. She motioned to the side, so I got out of the truck to see what was what.

We were all out there in the darkness with our flashlights in our 'jamas wandering around in the wilderness. Mom and I stood next to the cab with the driver's side door open and Dad paced back and forth by the picnic table, holding his lantern up high to get a better look. We could hear a rough, rumbling sound and Mom said I'd better get back in the truck. I took one step. Suddenly, there was a screech behind me, and Mom grabbed me by my britches and threw me into the truck so fast my face smashed against the passenger door. She jumped in, reached over me and started rolling up the window. Dad was right behind her, trying to get his window up and slam his door at the same time.

The truck was shifting and moaning and shaking. The lantern was lying out on the ground over by the picnic table. It looked like Dad had to made a quick evacuation. The truck really started to rock then, and I could hear the canvas roof tearing. No sooner had the ripping sounds stopped when something big started rolling around in the back of the truck. The two sides of the old topper were starting to cave in and stuff was flying around back there like a tornado had hit us. Whatever was back there was snarling and spitting and tearing up my stuff! I started to open my door; I had some pretty good stuff back there.

Dad yelled at me to get back in the truck, shut up and quit moving around. Out of the corner of my eye I can see a big, tan head in the rear window. His lips rolled up when he screeched, and he made a rumbling sound that lingered in the air when he was done yelling at us. It was some kind of a gigantic cat. He didn't look friendly. I thought I'd I seen one of these in a zoo a long time ago, eating half of a cow. This was not good!

The cat was all tangled up in the remains of our canvas roof. At some point, my dad's fishing rod got hooked up in the mess, and now whenever the cat tried to fight his way out, the fishing line and the rope that held our canvas in place kept tightening around his rear end. He stopped fighting every now and then, screeched some more, and then went back to the business at hand.

He wanted out of our truck, and we wanted him to get out of there, too. He had pretty much destroyed our camper and most of our stuff. The old cat was intent on retrieving the bag of leftover garbage that was strewn all over Mom 'n Dad's mattress, and he'd screech and hiss as he tried to drag himself toward his prey.

The brute kept rolling around back there, shifting the bed of the truck, and with every turn, he tightened the rope around the canvas. The madder he got, the more he rolled; the more he rolled, the more twisted up he became.

I glanced across the campground, searching for help. I could see the Girl Scouts were up and around, too. They must have heard the ruckus and were in the process of breaking camp at an all-time record speed. They grabbed their things, threw them into a fleet of waiting station wagons, formed a circle, and then drove off into the night. It didn't look like any help was coming from that end of the campground.

My dad's face was all screwed up, like he was trying to force some grand idea out the top of his head.

Mom came to the rescue. In a flurry of dumping her purse and searching through the glove box and then under the seat, she managed to come up with a flashlight that worked—and a big, sharp butcher knife.

She handed me the flashlight and told me to wait until I heard her open the truck door. Then I was supposed to shine the light right in the big cat's eyes through the back window.

When I heard the cab door groan, I clicked the switch. The light flooded the back of the camper and I could see my radio in a mangled heap on the floor of the truck bed. The cat looked right at me and jumped at the window in the back of the cab. Mom reached over the top of the camper, grabbed my dad's fishing pole, a loop of the rope and pulled the mess back into the cab of the truck. Then she slammed her door. She used her butcher knife to cut the rope and to release Dad's favorite fishing pole. She told my dad to close his mouth, open his eyes and start the engine.

The sound of the starter made the cat jump up on the cab of the truck. With the fishing line cut from the pole, the canvas began to unroll when the cat made the jump. He let out another screech and slid down the front window onto the hood of the truck. He didn't look as big now as he did when he was wearing the canvas outfit. His shoulders seemed to go up past his head when he walked, and he paced around back and forth in front of the truck. I guess he was wondering if he could still have the leftover chicken. Dad pressed on the horn, gave him a good blast, and the cat ran for cover up the cliff, finally disappearing behind a bunch of rocks.

Then silence. No one got out of the truck. No one said a word. We were all sitting there in our 'jamas, in disbelief, in the middle of nowhere. "This must be the quiet after the storm I always hear people talking about," I thought.

Dad put the truck into first gear and started creeping out of the campsite. We began to pick up speed and advanced toward the emergency exit. We headed down the mountain looking for an open gas station. Looking for an open anything, really, but it was the wee hours of the morning, and every building was shut up tight.

The remains of our homemade camper banged and slapped together as we drove. We just let them keep banging. Dad said they were already in such a shape that a little bit of knocking around wasn't going to hurt them now. He told us in no uncertain terms that no one would be getting out of the cab until we got somewhere with lights, or until the sun came up, which ever came first.

Come daylight, we would head back up the mountain and get whatever is left of our stuff. None of us seemed to be in much of a hurry to do that. Mom said she knew that was not a screech owl, and that Dad was full of beans when he tried to tell her it was. I was thinking I liked being the one that sleeps in the cab.

About a half an hour into our escape, we came upon an aluminum truck topper in the middle of some old man's yard with a "for sale" sign stuck to its window. It was used, but new to us, and a heck of a lot safer than the wounded fort we were carrying on the back of our truck.

Dad was interested in the new topper, and decided that things being what they were, he'd just go up to the house and wake the owner and try to buy the new camper for us. Mom and I waited in the truck while my dad explained our entire adventure in great detail to the old guy in the cowboy hat, who stood there in the door, looking like he was expecting us..

The man went on to say they had been having some trouble in the canyon lately, and they had to close the campsite this season. That explained why we were the only ones out there with good-smelling food. He took sympathy on our plight and gave us a good deal, whereupon we loaded the new topper onto the truck. He and my dad fastened it down and Dad left the plywood shell with the old man.

Back at the campsite with our new and improved equipment, we surveyed the damage. Not much left to gather up. The tent was down, Dad's fishing pole was never going to be the same, and my mom's good sweater was hanging from the top of an old dead tree.

We loaded up all our stuff, cleaned up the mess, then I climbed into the back of our new shiny shed, and we headed out of the mountains down to a kinder, friendlier, southern location.

Things didn't really turn out so bad. We finally got a real truck topper to use on vacations, I got a new radio, Mom got a new sweater, and Dad would have a great story to share from this adventure.

At every stop, in every town, in every state for the rest of our trip, we made sure to give him a lead-in so he could tell everyone about what he had hooked on his fishing line up in the mountains, and how glad we all were when it got away!

CHAPTER NINETEEN

The Crap in the CROCK

When you live in town, your milk comes in a red-and-white, wax-covered container. You keep it in the refrigerator and it is always clean and cold. I knew this, because when I went to school, they had smaller versions of these containers that they dispensed to all us kids at lunchtime. Getting the clean milk, as I called it, was my favorite part of every school day.

Out home we had milk, too. Sort of. It came from our cow, Bossy. Each morning, we had fresh milk, so to speak. Fresh milk meant that Mark or Dad had gone out to the barn early in the morning or just after supper, sat on a three-legged stool and done combat with the "*evil one*." No doubt she had kicked over the bucket a time or two, and maybe even kicked them as well. Bossy wouldn't go into the barn without a fight, bellowing and snorting through the whole process. Eventually, the good soldier would return to the house with a couple of buckets of warm, dirty-white milk and get it ready for the crock.

When the milk got to the house, it was peppered with shrapnel from the battlefield. The soldier would run it through a strainer to get all the big stuff out, and then pour it into a big crock on the counter on the back porch. After awhile a thick, slimy crust would form on the top of the milk. That was the cream, which we would scoop off and put in Mason jars in case the phone rang.

Remember I told you my dad had an aversion to telephones. He didn't want any teenagers hanging on it for hours, either. We only had one phone, placed strategically in the doorway between the kitchen and the living room. If you talked too long, the rest of the family would start an annoying parade from one room to the other, stepping on the curly cord or lifting it high above their heads and yanking the receiver out of your hand as they passed by.

The rule was whoever was talking on the phone had to make butter. As soon as the phone call came in, someone would run over to the 'fridge and grab a jar of cream. When it was determined the call was for you, they'd hand you the receiver in one hand and the butter jar in the other. It was a kind of a telephone timer of sorts. The whole time you talked, you were supposed to shake the jar hard enough to turn the cream to butter. If you stayed on the phone long enough to make two jars of butter, you would be in big trouble. Three jars and you knew you were in for some extra chores because it was obvious you had too much time on your hands. I never saw anyone make four jars of butter, but I heard tell of a time when Sharon was on her fourth jar, and it wasn't long after that she hit the road for her new life in the big city. You get the picture.

Anyway, the milk stayed on the counter on the back porch, in a big, old, ugly crock. The war-torn, dirty, stinky, slime-covered crock had a big copper ladle that hung right there on the side. The trick was to dip the ladle down deep in the milk and get it back out without getting anything else out but milk. I was pretty good at it most of the time, but then, even at my young age, I'd had a lot of milk dippin' experience.

When you finished getting all you needed, you had to stretch this thin piece of gray cloth over the top of the crock to prevent flies from drowning in the mess, and you had to be sure to wash the ladle or it would get pretty nasty, pretty fast.

Come evening, the contents of the big crock would be emptied into buckets and it would be washed out with soap and water. Dad would haul the leftover milk out to the barn lot, mix it with some slop for the hogs, finish feeding everything, go back to the battleground and produce another batch of milk for the crock. The whole ritual started over at daybreak. Someone in our family performed this deal every morning, every evening, every day, for every year we lived on the farm.

If we were going on a vacation, we had to find some other hardy soul to take to the battlefield against Bossy and retrieve the milk. People with the skills and fortitude to wage this type of war were not easy to come by, so we had to take all our vacation time at once so as not to deplete our reserves.

By the time I reached my thirteenth year, I'd tired of doing the same chores everyday at our place, and I wanted to spread my wings and do the same chores somewhere else. I'd built quite a reputation for baling hay, especially for a girl, and I got hired on with the crew over at Dickeys', our neighbors. I was as strong as most of the boys, worked cheap, and was available. Besides, every farm as far as the eye could see was baling at the same time. They were all looking for a warm body that could throw a seventy-pound bale over his or her head in the heat of a summer day.

The big farmer in the next town paid the highest wages, so he got his pick of the cream of the crop. The little farmers out our way had to settle for the leftovers. I was one of the better leftovers in the litter. The great thing about doing chores at someone else's place is that they pay you at the end of the day, right there next to the barn, in cash.

One evening, right after I came off my first day of hay baling employment, my $9.00 of cold, hard cash burned a hole in my pocket. I called home and had my mom come pick me up so we could go into town before I even cleaned up. I had business to do, a purchase to make.

She pulled the truck up along side the rack wagon and I jumped off the side and landed in the bed of the truck, I didn't have time to get into the cab. I leaned forward, stuck my head in her window and announced we were going up to Tindall's grocery store, because I needed to pick up something on the way home.

Mom never asked what I needed to buy; she just wheeled the old truck in behind the grocery. I jumped out of the back and headed into the store all by myself. I was a paying customer now. I didn't need to be wandering around waiting for my mom to get her stuff. I had cash. I was just like a grown-up. I walked right in, passed up the meat counter, flew by the cookie aisle, and didn't even glance at the candy spot. I just kept moving. When I got to the dairy aisle, I reached into the cooler and selected one half-gallon of fresh, cold, sanitized, homogenized, whole white milk!

Up to the checkout counter I went, trading my first dollar for the carton of milk and a big, fat, black marker. I grabbed my change and headed out for the truck. As soon as my butt hit the seat, I got out my marker and wrote my name on all four sides of the waxy container. No mistaking this—it is my milk. Mine! This milk belongs to me. It has my name all over it. I wrote "KEEP OUT" on one side, and then determined I might be becoming selfish, so I crossed it out. Besides, if I let my dad have some, maybe he'd come to his senses about the crap in the crock he thinks is real milk. Maybe then we can start getting this good stuff all the time.

Beneath the scribbled out "KEEP OUT" sign, I wrote "Try it, you'll love it!" I was pretty sure this was a new product for my parents—they'd just never had the chance to try it before.

Mom never let on if she was surprised with my purchase. We drove back to the farm in silence, she was watching the road, and I was watching my milk. Soon as we pulled into our parking spot, I ran for the house. Before the screen door slammed behind me, I had the refrigerator open and I was cleaning out a space for my milk. I shoved all the leftovers down to lower shelves, got me a dishrag and wiped off the top shelf. I placed my carton right in the middle, just under the little light. I turned the carton around so Dad would be sure and see the part about trying out the milk from a carton. I was sure he'd be thrilled with his first taste of the good stuff! He'd be coming in pretty soon for some lemonade and then he'd find my good milk, instead! Won't he be surprised?! I was excited! This was going to be great!

I stepped back and evaluated my display. I grabbed the metal pitcher of lemonade and dumped it down the kitchen drain. I didn't want any competition on the shelves today. That big old metal pitcher was taking up way to much space. Besides, Dad wasn't going to want any of that old, bitter lemonade when he could have fresh, cold, sanitized, homogenized milk.

I could hear my dad coming in from the barn. He reached the sidewalk, carrying two buckets of that crap he wanted to pour in the crock. I ran over and took my normal spot at the table. I wanted to see his face when he found my milk in the refrigerator! I was so excited my knees bounced up and down under the table; I even had to sit on my hands to keep them under control.

Dad seemed to be taking forever to dump his load. He was just messing around with that awful old milk. I couldn't stand the suspense, and felt like I would explode any second. I bit my bottom lip to keep from giving away my surprise.

An eternity later, after he got his milk strained and put the rag back on the top of the old gray crock, he went to the cupboard and got a glass for his lemonade and wandered over to the 'fridge. My moment of glory was almost there. I let out a little squeal. Any second now, he was going to see what I'd done! "Come on, Dad, open that door!" I pleaded silently.

The door gave off a sucking sound when he pulled on the handle. A gleam of light spilled out into the kitchen. I held my breath. Dad just stood there with his arm on the door, beholding the sight of a new milk carton. He was speechless.

Now my dad smoked like a chimney and swore like a sailor every day. He couldn't say "the" without adding a swear word to it. So his first reaction didn't even faze me.

"Who in the heck is buying milk around here?" Only he didn't really say "heck."

"I did, Daddy, with my own money!" I sat up a little taller; my pride was starting to show. "I had Mom drive me all the way into town just so I could get you some real milk." By then, I wasn't only being prideful, but was outright bragging about my new-found wealth and all the power that comes with having money.

"I throw out gallons of milk every single day and you decide to go into town and buy milk?" He was in shock at his good fortune, I could tell. He's thinking what a great kid I am, I'm sure. It was obvious to me this was an emotional moment for him, and I should ease him into this newfound lifestyle of luxury.

"Well, Daddy, I thought you might never have tried any real milk." I said, as sweetly as I could. There, I'd put that out there pretty well. I hadn't said anything that would hurt his feelings. I was being careful not to insinuate it might be that we were poor.

"What in the heck do you think we get from that cow out there in the damn barn day after day? Why do you think they call it a 'milk cow'? What in the heck were you thinking?" he said, his voice a mixture of astonishment, anger and something I couldn't quite put my finger on.

Okay, I was starting to get the picture. I didn't really think he wanted me to answer the question. Change is hard for anybody, 'n apparently finding a carton of milk in his 'fridge was just a little over the top for my dad. Maybe I should've just gotten the quart size for our first time. "Dad should try this stuff before he decides he doesn't like it," I thought. I mentioned that they sold butter at the store, too. I thought maybe he didn't know.

"Now what in the heck happened to my lemonade? What in God's green earth is going on around here? There is not one single cold thing to drink in this God forsaken place!" he hollered.

I decided not to mention there was cold MILK in there!

Dad fumbled in his pocket, produced a beat-up, bent-up pack of cigarettes, staggered over to his seat at the table and flopped down. He lit one up, and stared out the front window with a glazed look over his face. His hands were trembling. A few minutes passed and he turned his face my way, trying to recap the day's events. He cleared his throat and his voice cracked. "Let me see if I have this right. You leave me with all your chores so you can take on a job over at Dickeys' balin' hay. Then you work all day 'n get paid. As soon as you have money in your pocket, you talk your mom into drivin' you all the way in town so's you can pay cold hard cash for milk in a carton! Meanwhile, I am hauling buckets of the stuff out to the pigs because no one 'round here drinks it. Is that about right?"

Yep, that was pretty much it, but he forgot the part about the milk being sanitized, homogenized and in a waxed carton. You know, when it comes to milk, presentation is everything.

CHAPTER TWENTY

Breakin' Up is HARD TO DO

When I was a freshman, something exciting happened at our high school. From somewhere we'd acquired a trampoline, a balance beam and some parallel bars. This was the most important thing that had happened in our town in some time. Everybody was talking about it.

I was a prime choice to work on the uneven parallel bars. All summer long, I'd been baling hay and we had a trapeze bar that hung from a tree over the gully that I played on all of the time. I was thin, flexible, and strong. Our gym teacher kept telling us that what we needed to be good at the parallel bars was upper body strength, and I had some.

I was so excited to find something I could be good at that I worked overtime to see what all I could do. Our teacher had shown me how to do this neat trick, where you got up some steam, bounced off the lower beam, let go of the top bar, turned around in mid-air, and caught the top beam on your way back down. I was sure the secret to doing a good job was to build up lots of steam and really whack that bottom bar when you were starting the routine. I wanted to get some height!

Our class had been working out on the bars for a few months, and when it got close to Christmas time, the school was going to put on a display to show off the new stuff. I'd been chosen to be the show-off on the parallel bars. I practiced every gym class and study hall, and stayed after school to get every opportunity to learn my routine. I came in early and I left late. I wanted to be a BIG show-off. This was going to be my moment in the sun, the fifteen minutes of fame I'd waited for all 14 years of my life.

The day before the program, I had a pass to get out of most of my classes, so I was down in the gym bouncing and swinging to my heart's content. I was enjoying my stardom and the fact that I didn't have to give up my turn and let anyone else on. Right then, I was special.

The gym teacher spent most of her day with me, giving me pointers and having me add and subtract different parts of the routine. She timed each segment to make sure we had everything just right, down to the last second. Then we worked on the dismount. Finally, she pronounced I was ready!

That afternoon, there was to be an assembly. Six people were going to be doing demonstrations on the new equipment, and my act was the finale. We all wore matching garb, blue with thin white stripes, and I had the feeling that I was really going to be the star!

After each of the first five acts, everyone in the gym stomped their feet on the bleachers and clapped. They cheered and smiled. I couldn't wait to see what they were going to do once they saw the show I was going to put on!

Time crawled by, but finally, it was my turn. I took my running jump, grabbed the top bar and was on my way! Things were going great, not one mistake in the first minute of my routine. I was born to fly! Each time I bounced off the bottom bar, it would moan. I remember thinking, "That's different," but maybe it was just because I was doing such a fine job. I kept going. My big moment came toward the end of the routine. It was the part where I needed to let go of the top bar for just a moment and turn around in mid-air. I hit the bottom bar just as I let go of the top… there was a crackling sound, a rumble and a moan, and the bottom bar split and broke, sending me crashing into the set of bleachers that were still closed up along the side of the gym wall.

Hitting the wall that hard had knocked the wind out of me, and plenty of people came running over to see how badly I was hurt. The teachers got this big neck roll thing and put it around my neck and called my folks and an ambulance. When I heard that an ambulance was coming, I thought I must have been hurt and just didn't know it. I decided to play the part. I moaned and winced, and tried to look pitiful.

Now the "calling my parents" deal might not have been the best option for me. My folks didn't like having to come up to the school for anything, and they liked doctors even less. We'd been told from the time we could walk that if we ever got into trouble at school, it would be nothing compared to what would happen to us when we got home.

I was still lying there on the floor with the neck roll when I heard the side door to the gym open; I knew that my mom had come in. I couldn't see her. I was still staring up at the ceiling, and I couldn't move my head to the side because of the neck roll thing, but I could hear her distinctive walk. "Clickity, clop, clickity, clop, clickity, clop-d-clop-d-clop." It was my mom all right.

Everyone with any authority whatsoever started talking to her at once, trying to tell her what had happened. I was going to get some sympathy now! Did she hear the part about flying across the gym? Did she catch that piece about the bar snapping? It wasn't my fault, you know … faulty bar. I was going to get to go to a hospital in an ambulance! Wonder if she caught that? I'm not sure, but I might have been smiling.

Mom just kept heading in my direction. Her footsteps were louder now, but followed the same familiar beat. "Clickity, clop, clickity, clop, clickity, clop-d-clop-d-clop." Then everyone stopped talking. Footsteps stopped clicking. The background noise was gone.

The gym teacher whispered to Mom that she didn't think anyone should move me until the ambulance came.

Mom was standing right over me now. I could see her face bent over my prone body, looking me up and down, hands on her hips. She was still wearing her coveralls with the work gloves hanging out of the pockets; she must have been clean out in the barn when they called her. That couldn't have been good.

"Are you hurt?" she asked me.

Well, to be truthful, I hadn't given it much thought. I was pretty interested in what everyone else was saying and doing, and hadn't really noticed that nothing really hurt. I wiggled my fingers and toes, moved one arm, and decided I'd better answer the question.

"No, m'am… I don't think so."

"Well, then, get up off that floor. You look like a darn fool lying there," she said in a no-nonsense voice.

I could hear the murmurs of the teachers' voices, trying

to determine if she was insane or if she didn't understand exactly what had happened.

I tried to look out the corners of my eyes to see if I could figure out what I should do next. Finally Mom spoke again.

"Do you hurt anywhere? Quit looking out the side of your head, your neck works, doesn't it? You had these fine people call me all the way in here and there isn't a thing wrong with you. Now get up!"

So I did. I stood up, handed the fancy neck roll back to the gym teacher and followed my mom out to the truck. We passed the ambulance along the road on the way back to the farm. Guess I didn't need it anyway.

Mom gave me the lecture about "when you need an ambulance, you'll know it" and murmured something about me probably needing one the next time they call her up to the schoolhouse for no good reason. There was also something in there about if people were meant to fly, they'd grow wings.

That day I found out that just because a bunch of people are running around in lots of directions, telling you you're hurt bad, doesn't necessarily mean they know more about it than you do. It's okay to get help when you're hurt; it's not okay to pretend you're hurt just to get attention. Mostly I learned that my mom loved me enough to come in from the field, drive all the way to the schoolhouse to make sure I was just acting, and forgive me when she found out I was.

CHAPTER TWENTY 1

Smokey 'n the LAKE

Even as a child, I wanted to impress people. I wanted them to pay attention to me. Once I thought I had it all worked out so that I'd leave an impression on a prospective companion, a fella I wanted to remember me forever. I left an impression all right. I'm pretty sure he could tell you this story better than I can.

I was fourteen, and what I really wanted was to find a guy who might be interested in me. Just down the road from our farm a new subdivision was being built around a little pond they were planning to turn into a lake. The development group had been digging around in there and now it was deep enough for boats, so they had hired a lifeguard to keep all of us kids out of there while they were building the roads and a beach. Of course I had to go down to investigate.

The lifeguard's name was Rick. He was about 19 or 20 and drove a rusty old black Jeep with the top sawed off. He was tall, tan and blonde and had big, sparkling white teeth. He'd be quite a catch, and I was determined to be the "catcher."

One early fall morning, I got up with the sun, went out to the barn lot and saddled up Smoke. Smoke was my favorite horse; he was gray with a long black mane and tail. He had a fire in his spirit that shone in his eyes, and looked like one of the stallions you always see in pictures, the ones with the wind-blown mane, and tufts of steam snorting from their nose.

On this day I wanted Smoke to look his best, so I dug up our black dress saddle and my favorite Indian blanket. I even took a bedroll, saddlebags and a canteen in case I got lucky!

It was the late sixties, and I'd dressed myself in full sixties garb. I had on low-cut jeans, a bikini top, red cowboy boots, a leather coat with fringes down both arms, and had fixed my long, dark hair into one single braid and put a headband around my forehead, Indian style.

Just as I reached the cliff overlooking the lake, a beam of sunshine fell on me, and I saw Rick the lifeguard pull up in his Jeep. I waved at Rick and Rick waved at me... I was thinking of how wonderful I had to look, sitting there in the sunbeam. I knew I had Rick's attention now!

What happened next I will NEVER get over! Just as I moved the reins to turn Smoke toward the path leading down to the beach, a bunch of ugly birds flew out of some brush and Smoke lurched forward, jumping off the cliff into 20 feet of water!

It was NOTHING like you see on the movies! I hung on for dear life. When Smoke hit the water, it was like I'd done a giant belly flop. It felt like someone had hit me across the forehead with a baseball bat. I must have been screaming all the way down, because my nose, mouth and lungs were full of water. I came up once for air, and a moment later went under again. My boots were filled with water. One foot had slipped though the stirrup, so every time Smoke came up out of the water, I went under. That wet leather coat seemed to weigh about 500 pounds; I had to let it go. As the saddle became waterlogged, it slipped sideways, and then I was under the water almost all the time. Everything I'd ever learned about swimming became null and void at this point.

Rick the lifeguard was my only hope. He never even came near the water to save me.

I finally kicked off the boot that was holding me under, and Smoke dragged us through mud two feet deep up to the side of the lake.

When we reached the edge, I lay there in the mud, puffing and panting. I reached up and grabbed the stirrup so the horse wouldn't get away. Then my not-so-valiant steed did this horse-shudder thing, the cinch broke, the saddle fell on top of me, and the saddle horn whacked me on the forehead. When I opened my eyes, I was lying less than three feet away from wonderful Rick.

Smoke bolted for home, leaving me with the mess.

So there I was, covered in mud, missing a boot, dragging a broken saddle, and growing a goose egg on my forehead. I sat up, coughed up some water and slime, and tried to scrape off a few layers of mud.

Rick—my HERO—just stood there with his hair on his head, his teeth in his mouth and his jaw dragging the ground, not saying a word. Guess he forgot he was suppose to be the lifeguard.

Finally, an old guy (who was probably 35) from the construction site got a hose and rinsed me off with freezing water. Then I began my long journey home.

I don't know why, but I walked all the way with one boot on, one off. It made this squishing sound with every other step—clump, squish, drag... clump, squish, drag... all the way home. The saddle was heavy, but I never considered leaving it behind.

That day was an important lesson to me in many ways—I learned that trying to impress people never turns out the way you plan it. People you count on to save you don't always jump in when you need them. Even when you are going under for the third time, keep fighting; you might still make it out. Most importantly, I learned that no matter how heavy the load or how far the journey, take what you have left all the way home.

CHAPTER TWENTY 2

Apples in my POCKET

I wanted Smoke to be like other people's horses. I wanted to walk out to the barn lot and have him come running up to me, nuzzle my face and wait impatiently for me to ride him.

Smoke had a different plan. His scheme involved me chasing him around the barn lot and gully for forty-five minutes, cornering him by a fence, grabbing his mane, holding his head tightly while I put the bit in his mouth, and then waiting while I puffed and panted to catch my breath before we went for a ride. I rode that horse pretty much every day for ten years, and everyday it was the same thing.

One year, I decided the reason he kept running from me was that I didn't bring him treats. So, every morning, I'd steal carrots from the 'fridge or corn from the crib. By fall, he was used to me bringing apples from the orchard. I always had treats when I came near him.

Because we lived on the farm, I had this old brown coat with huge pockets. I'd wander out to the orchard, pick up apples until the pockets were full, and then visit Smoke, letting him find them. The pockets of this coat were wide and deep, and Smoke could put his face in, feel around for the apples, and then pick them out one at a time. It took a while, but he finally got to the point that he'd come to me when he saw me jump the gate, and I loved it. He still ran when he saw the bit, and we still had to do the forty-five minute dance every time, but at least he'd check me out to see if I had treats first.

One morning, there was a big tussle in the barn lot. I was up at the house and could hear my Dad's voice, and lots of screamin' 'n hollerin'. Smoke let out some pretty loud noises too, and then I saw him come running through the gully like his tail was afire.

Dad was out in the lane, walking with a limp, rubbing his rear end with one hand, and holding the other hand over his ear.

I hurried out to the lane to see what was up. "What have you been teaching that darn horse of yours?" Dad wanted to know, and he wanted to know now!

"I don't know. Same old stuff," I answered, not wanting to give away any of my training secrets.

"Well, he's getting mean, and we aren't going to keep him if he is going to be biting people." By now, Dad was a few steps up ahead of me, and I could see the back pocket had been torn off his jeans, and he was missing a big piece of the butt of his pants, too. His ear was swollen and he was covered in cow poop. He looked bad and smelled worse.

Dad went on to say he had just come up from the field and had decided to go over to the orchard to see how the apples were coming along. He had picked up a few and put them in his hind pocket. When he climbed over the fence, Smoke had run over to him, bit the pocket right off his butt, and knocked him down off the gate! Dad had given Smoke a good kick, and Smoke had returned the favor, which is why my father was limping. When the horse kicked him, Dad had landed in a pile of manure, and a wasp had come by and stung him on the ear. Dad said he was going in the house to get another pair of jeans and to put some lard on his ear, and told me in no uncertain terms that I'd better figure out what I was going to do about *that* horse.

It was one of those times when I had to come clean. I told Dad not to sell the horse, that I'd been feeding him apples from my pocket, trying to get him to like me better. Dad decided the carrots and corn and apples were okay, but I couldn't let him find them in my pockets. Someone could get hurt bad, like him, for instance.

I started feeding Smoke treats from over the fence in the gully, and I didn't let him fetch them from my pockets anymore, which took a lot of the fun out of the whole deal.

It was safe for Dad to pick apples when he came in from the fields, but I noticed he always looked for Smoke before he came over the fence. I don't know why he was so mad about the whole deal; at least he got a new pair of jeans.

Then Smoke had the best of both worlds. He was still getting treats, but he had the fence as a safety shield between us. He knew full well he could get away easily, and that unless I jumped the fence, there was no chance he was going to have to take me for a ride. He also had my Dad trained to bring extra apples when he came from the orchard. Dad would throw the extras to the other side of the lot while he crossed over the fence. And Smoke still got to dance with me for forty-five minutes every day. Our dance started out more of a tango, and over time, evolved into a ballet. Smoke was a remarkable teacher.

CHAPTER Twenty 3

Losin' A LOAD

At our house, doing the laundry was a big deal. We didn't have a washer and dryer at home, so once a week, Mom and I went into town to do the laundry

As soon as I got off the school bus, my mom would be waiting at the corner of our lane in the truck. She'd have all the baskets of dirty clothes in the back with towels tucked down over the top of each basket and we would head off to the laundromat.

It would be a girls' night out. We would wash all the clothes, grab ice cream from the shop next door, get candy and orange pop out of a vending machine, and pick up groceries before we made our way home. Once in a while in the summer, we would even stop at the drive-in movie to see a show. Mom and I always had a great time on laundry day.

I especially liked doing the laundry itself, well, just the folding really. I loved getting the towels out of the dryers while they were still warm and rubbing them up against my face, breathing in the clean, sweet smell of Tide. We would fold the whole bunch, separate the tidy piles into her basket, his basket, my basket, and the towel basket, and then tuck a towel over each one so the wind wouldn't mess things up in the bed of the truck. Then we'd load all the baskets and off we'd go toward home.

Mom was like a mailman. Neither rain nor snow nor hail…prevented her from making the regular weekly laundry run. We always went the same night of the week, always to the same place, once a week, for all the years I lived at home. No one ever suggested or entertained the idea of getting a washer and dryer for the house. I don't think our well would have handled it anyway. It was just understood that we would be going into town that one night and we wouldn't be home in time to make supper.

One particular day, things started off poorly and turned uglier as the night went on. As soon as we got to the outskirts of town in the truck, it started raining cats 'n dogs. We didn't have the topper on the truck then, so all our dirty clothes got wet. It made them heavy to lug in to the laundromat, and Mom said we had to do them anyway, because now they were all wet and we didn't have any way to dry them out at home. Mom was having a bad night. That evening, something was wrong with the big silver washers she always liked to use, and she had to settle for the normal ones. She overloaded one, and soap and water ran out all over the floor. That didn't make her happy. Something red got in with the whites and left everything that sad pink color. She lost some dimes in the dryers and that ticked her off, but by the time things were dry and folded, she decided that life was smelling sweeter again all around. The clothes were clean, the rain had passed, and the world was right once more.

The bed of the truck was still a little damp, but Mom decided we could go ahead and put the stuff back there anyway. It was always so crowded if we had to ride with it stacked on my side in the truck's cab, and the sky looked pretty clear by then. So, out there in the laundromat parking lot under the streetlights, we loaded all of our clothes into the back of the truck, towels tucked in place to keep everything secure, groceries stacked strategically to prevent fallout, and with ice cream in our possession, we started our long journey back to the farm. We were running late, but it didn't seem to matter much. After all, the laundry was done.

As usual, my mom and I talked all the way home. We laughed about the washing machine spilling soapy water out on the floor, and the way the owner of the laundromat ran around trying to sop up the water. We joked about other things that had happened to us that day. We enjoyed just driving along and shooting the breeze, windows down, hair flying, eating our ice cream, on a nice cool fall night.

Then Mom looked up in the rear view mirror, turned a pale shade of gray, and pulled over to the side of the road. She flung open the driver's door and got out of the truck without saying a word. I scrambled out my side to see what the matter was. There in the back of the truck bed was … nothing. No groceries, no clothes, no laundry baskets, it was empty, clean. We'd left the tailgate down on the truck. We'd lost our load.

Mom slammed the tailgate into its rightful position, got back in the truck, whipped it around, and we headed back into town. It was dark now, and every piece of litter along the road looked like something we might have lost. She'd slow down, examine it, try to determine if it was a discarded grocery bag or Dad's jeans, and then send me out to inspect it and make a final decision. This went on for the entire eleven miles back to the laundromat. We found a shirt here, a sock there. Jeans were the hardest to spot because they were dark and it was night by now. We found the sugar and flour, but they were not salvageable. Mom was mostly concerned with where her underpants might have ended up. Something about someone else finding her underwear really upset her.

We searched all the way into town, and all the way back. Those were the longest twenty-two miles I'd ever traveled. I don't think she ever got the truck out of first gear. We were just a couple of people creeping along the highway in a beat-up truck, in search of our groceries and our undies.

Over the next several hours, we finally found all of the laundry baskets, some of the groceries, and part of our clothes. We couldn't find all the underwear, but we had most of it, enough to get us by. As the night wore on, Mom finally determined we'd found all we were going to find, and it was time to take what we had left and make the best of it.

The following week, laundry day moved up a day or two. We headed straight for a store to replace some of our missing clothes before we went on to do the wash. All the way into town, we watched to see if we could spot anything that belonged to us along the ditches.

Just as we rounded Dead Man's Curve, there it was. Mom's biggest fear, hanging right there out in the open for the world to see—one pair of big, old, holey, slightly pink underpants, neatly stretched out and hanging between two branches of Miller's oak tree. You could tell someone had found them along the road and had decided to make a display. They were flapping in the breeze and seemed to be waving us down as we went by.

"Mom! Right there! There are some of your underpants!" I shouted and pointed, pretty excited that we'd found more of the laundry. "Stop, and I'll jump out and get 'em!"

Mom hunkered down behind the steering wheel and stepped on the gas.

"Slow down! I am pretty sure them panties must be ours!" I was totally caught off guard. What is she doing? We'd scoured the countryside for days looking for our belongings, and for some freaky reason, now she was speeding up to pass them by!

My mom stared straight ahead and refused to even glance over to check them out and see if they were hers. I'd have continued to protest, but she had that "don't-say-another-word" look in her eye and was biting her bottom lip. She shifted into high gear and tromped the accelerator to the floor. The truck gasped for air and was running at full force. We took that curve at break-neck speed. It was plain to see that my mom was afraid of her own underwear! She rounded the corner, and just as we passed the tree, she let off the gas, the truck heaved a sigh of relief, and began to slow down to our regular sedate, goof-around speed. I let go of the dash, sat back in my seat, and watched as my knuckles started to regain their natural color.

It was obvious to me that I should not mention the panties in the tree to my dad, or anyone else for that matter, if I wanted to continue to be a part of the family.

From that day forward, laundry day was never the same. We still had the laundry in the back of the truck; we still made a night of it. We still had a his basket, a her basket, my basket, and the towel basket. We also added one small extra basket—the undies basket. It always rode in the front of the cab, right on the front seat, right between us. And it made it home safe 'n sound every time.

CHAPTER TWENTY 4

My First DATE

The First Date! Everybody has one. Well, almost everybody. They never seem to come off the way we expect. For all our planning and primping, it seems like everything that can go wrong, does. In my case, plenty did. In fact, so many things went so wrong, I wish I'd just stayed at home.

My first date came with lots of fanfare. I knew two weeks in advance, and had called my sister, Sharon, who lived in Chicago, for advice. She was ten years my senior, and I thought she'd know all the things a girl should do to win a guy's heart.

Her advice was "don't be loud, be careful to laugh in a lady-like fashion, and be sure to keep your dress tucked in when you sit down." These were pretty tall orders for me, as I was always loud, never wore dresses, and laughed a lot like a donkey.

She even sent a dress down for me to wear that she felt would be appropriate for a young lady on her first date.

When the big day came, I dressed up in my new attire, had my hair done at a beauty parlor for the first time in my life, and then added the final touch—straight teeth.

I'd had an accident out on the farm and all of my front teeth had been kicked out the year before, so I'd gotten false teeth at the early age of fifteen. When my original set was made, the dentist wanted them to look "natural" and put a crooked tooth in the front, just like my real ones had been. I always hated them. My parents splurged that year and had a different plate made—with all straight teeth. The day of my first date, I'd gone into town and picked up the new teeth. I was sure the straight new teeth would make me so fascinating that David, the boy who had my attention, wouldn't be able to take his eyes off of me!

My date arrived at 4:30 p.m. I remember being up in my room, admiring my teeth, when my mother came up to tell me he was in the front room. Mom made sure I had my old teeth in a soapbox in my purse, just in case. I ran downstairs at a break-neck speed to embark on the most embarrassing evening of my entire life.

David, my date, and I arrived at the movies right on time. We were there to watch a Disney movie, a comedy, and I kept reminding myself NOT to laugh like a donkey. The next thing I knew, something funny happened on the screen and I let out a bellow that made the rafters shake. To my surprise, my beautiful new teeth flew out of my mouth and landed two aisles ahead of us in a fat woman's lap. It was dark in the movie theater, so the lady fumbled in her lap for the flying object, lifted it close to her face and began to scream as she flung them up against a concrete wall.

David was all concerned with the antics going on up front, and I was wondering what I was going to tell my parents about my missing teeth, not to mention that I could not let HIM see ME without my pearly whites!

I mumbled something about having to go to the ladies room, where I opened the soap dish my mother had put in my bag. There, between the plastic covers, were my old teeth, covered in petroleum jelly, all slimy and gross. Sitting in one of the stalls, I tried to wipe off the goop with toilet paper but it kept sticking to the pink plastic. Finally, I decided it was the best I could do and stuck them in my mouth.

After the show, we went to get a pizza, and all David could talk about was the fat lady who had to leave the show because she was so upset that someone had thrown something at her. He wondered what it was that had landed in her lap. I was in a hurry to change the topic, or at least to suggest other objects that might have hit her…popcorn, candy, gum… when the pizza finally came.

As soon as the waitress set the pizza on the table, I grabbed a slice and stuck it in my mouth, thinking that I wouldn't be expected to talk with my mouth full. But the pizza was hot! So hot I had to yank it out, only to see my old teeth stuck to the top of the pizza!

Now, what does a young lady say on her first date in a situation like this? It's not like you can deny the teeth are yours. Nothing my mother had lectured me on the week before had prepared me for this! I did the only thing I could think of—I stuck the whole thing, pizza, teeth and all, back into my mouth. Then, in the most casual way I could, I tried to use my tongue to pry my teeth away from the melted mess. The whole time, David just stared at me. He never moved or uttered a single word.

We didn't eat the rest of the pizza; I guess one piece was enough. David drove me home and dumped me out on the driveway. He didn't even say goodnight.

I never got my new teeth back, but I always wondered what the guy who cleans up after the show thought when he found their remains, and what kind of the story the fat lady had to tell to her grandchildren! "I was sitting at a theater, minding my own business, watching a Disney movie, when all of a sudden there was this donkey behind me and ..."

As for me, life went on, although I was sure it would never be the same. I didn't want to go back to school, but I had to. I didn't ever want to see David again, but I had to. I didn't want to have false teeth anymore, but the alternative was even less appealing, so I had to do that, too.

Someone once said, "You wouldn't worry about what people thought about you if you knew how seldom they do." I don't know. I have a hard time believing there aren't some other people around who still think about that night!

As for the first-date-advice I got from my sister? She was absolutely right. The whole night was going along fine until I got loud and forgot to laugh in a lady-like fashion!

CHAPTER TWENTY 5

One Bad Cat ~ THOMAS

Out in our barn, we always had a big clan of cats. Big ones, little ones, black ones, white ones, fancy oriental ones, and calicos. They were all strays, and they were all pretty scrappy.

People from town would like the little kittens, but when they grew into big cats, they weren't quite as loveable. The townspeople would sneak out to our place at night and leave the grown cats by the side of the road. Cats aren't stupid, and sooner or later, they'd make their way into the barn looking for some fresh milk come milking time.

We didn't mind much. The cats kept the vermin population under control and we didn't have to feed them very often. None of them ever came near the house, and they all seemed to take care of one another.

Over time, we ended up with one big pack of cats and one loner cat. The old loner cat came to be known as Thomas, and he was one ugly cat. He had black, matted fur in most places; in other places he was bald. He had one eye that was permanently closed. The top part of his left ear was missing, and he walked kind of sideways with a limp. There was a huge scar over his behind, and it looked like the fur around the scar was trying to come in white.

Thomas had been living out in our barn for more than a year, and he seemed to be doing a fine job of keeping the rats out of the corncrib. Whenever he came out of the barn, every animal in the lot took notice. Chickens ran for the safety of their coop, goats headed down the lane to the woods, horses fled the barn lot for the gully, and even Bossy would raise her head and acknowledge his presence.

Thomas could start a sheep stampede just by walking up behind them and letting out his snarl. Both of our collies were terrified of him—the mere sight of his face could make them turn tail and head for the hills. This sure was one ornery old cat!

As Thomas got older he seemed to need a little more interaction. Every once in a while, when I was lying on the bales of hay in the barn, he'd sneak over and make his bed next to mine. On a good day, he'd let me pet his stiff, old, mangy fur. We seemed to have an unspoken understanding. I didn't pet him unless he asked for it, and he didn't bite me unless I asked for it. We got along fine.

I heard him purr once, and it sounded more like an old engine that was missing on a few cylinders than like a cat. I came to have respect for his war wounds and stopped worrying about the way he looked.

As time passed, Thomas decided that we were friends. He'd meet me at the door each time I entered the barn. Sometimes he'd even rub against my leg to let me know he was glad to see me. I'd bring him a treat now and then.

Come fall, I wasn't out there as much. I had school and all, and Dad was picking up some of my duties so I could spend time on my studies. Thomas started to miss me.

That fall, Thomas began to come clear up to the house at night. When he figured out which room I was in, all of a sudden, there'd be a loud bang, I'd look up, and there he'd be, hanging by his front claws from the top of the windowsill. I'd wave at him, acknowledge his presence, and then he'd slowly slide down the glass and disappear into the darkness once again. I guess it was his way of reminding me that I was neglecting him.

He got pretty good at hanging onto the windowsills. Occasionally, I'd be eating supper and get that funny feeling someone was watching me. I'd start to glance around at the glass openings, and there he'd be, head just over the sill, peeking in with his one good eye to see what we were doing.

When the worst of the winter set in, I took pity on Thomas and started letting him into the house at night. When it came time to go to bed, he'd jump up on the back door and hang on the sill of the glass. I'd open the door and he'd bolt inside, stop to hiss at the dogs, run up the stairs, and scoot under my bed.

In the morning, when I went down for breakfast, he'd wait until he heard the door open, come flying down the steps as fast as he could go, stop and hiss at the dogs, then hit the door at break-neck speed, and head back out to the barn for his food.

Mom didn't like Thomas, and Thomas didn't like my mom. If she tried to be nice to him, he'd hiss and bow his back. He didn't need anyone else fussing over him. He was happy with things just the way they were, thank you very much. Thomas was proud; he didn't want her fancy leftovers, unless she put them in a bowl for the dogs. Then they became the object of his intense affection; he was willing to fight for the very last bite. It was the principle of the thing. If it was good enough for the dogs, it was good enough for Thomas.

One night, as Thomas hung on the glass of the kitchen door and I walked over to let him in, another big old cat jumped up out of the darkness and onto the porch. Thomas slid down the glass, arched his back and let out a howl that made the windows shutter. The stranger's cat backed up into the opposite corner of the porch and put on his attack face. There was going to be one big cat fight.

I turned on the porch light so we could get a better look. The stranger's cat was putting up a good struggle, but Thomas was hanging in there. Fur flew all over the porch, at one time, the air was so thick with fur you couldn't even see the light bulb on the ceiling. Both cats were experienced warriors and neither was willing to give an inch.

Dad reached over and opened the drawer in the kitchen that was filled with firecrackers. We used them to scare dogs off our place when they were chasing our sheep. He lit one long string, threw open the screen door, and tossed them out on the porch. They seemed to pop on for a few minutes, then both cats let out one last yowl, and things started to settle down.

The stranger's cat took off and Thomas came limping into the house. I knew it had been a tough fight because he didn't even stop to hiss at the dogs. He just slowly dragged himself up the steps and crawled up on the end of my bed.

It was right there on the end of my bed that Thomas died. I guess the fight was more than he could handle.

After that night, Dad started reciting a poem about Thomas. I was never sure if he had written it, or if it was one he learned when he was a kid, but this is how it goes:

Old farmer white
had a big black cat,
That was stiff with age,
and blind as a bat.

And he'd often said
to his eldest son,
We'll keep old Thomas
for the good he's done.

He's killed more rats,
and fought more strange and thieving cats,
than any cat in the county round,
and besides, his equal cannot be found.

Then along came a stranger's cat one night,
intent on plunder and chucked full of fight.
He gave a yowl in the midnight gloom,
which aroused old Thomas in the sitting room.

He sharpened his claws,
and he bowed his back,
and calmly awaited
the stranger's attack.

The fight began with an awful roar,
they each had fought many times before.
They snipped and they snarled
the tail of the other, the other one clawed.

They made such a loud and infernal noise,
that the farmer yelled for the oldest boy,
then he reached around for the old bootjack,
and the stranger's cat got an awful whack
which doubled him up in the small of his back
and sent him off on the homeward track.

But, nay, when the farmer rose at the break of day,
there on the floor old Thomas lay.
He vowed that he'd hunt for a thousand years,
and catch that other cat by the ears,
and punch his liver out through his chest,
no lesser act would give him rest.

But when his rage began to cool,
he called himself a darned old fool.
For fate had served him right.
He shouldn't 've let old Thomas fight.

Guess Dad pretty much said it all.

Epilogue

It wasn't long after Thomas died that I graduated from high school and moved off the farm. My folks stayed on another twenty-five years or so. After my Dad died, Mom said it was never the same, and she traded Mark the farm for a house in town. The old "homestead" has since been passed on in the family, and from time to time, I get out there to take a peek at the changes that have taken place over the years.

Each time I show up, I am given a tour of all the improvements, and each time I leave thinking how much it stays the same.

Once, about ten years ago, I had a hair-brained idea that it would be great to move back out that way again. I wanted to take my turn at buying the old place and finishing the job that my folks had started so long ago. I had my husband hoodwinked into thinking we could do it, too. Then, one rainy spring afternoon I decided to take a walk out into our old woods. I loaded up a canvas bag and tried to walk back in time. Mud and leaves stuck to my good leather loafers, and my sweater was getting ruined by the brambles and briars that grabbed at my shoulders. No livestock lived on the place anymore, and the weeds were taking over the woods and the barnyard. The farm seemed smaller now, and less romantic. I wondered about getting out of the lane during the winters, and how to get a deep well closer to the house. I didn't like the idea of the work it would take to get the out buildings in good shape, and I was thinking how much I'd miss the comforts and conveniences of living in the cities.

By the end of my walk, I knew I'd never be moving back to that life. I headed up the lane, cut through the orchard and walked up my old route to the hay barn. Over in the horse stall, I saw a pair of my old gray coveralls hanging next to side door. I lifted them off the nail and Smoke's bridle fell to the floor. I buried my head in my hands and cried.

It was there in the shadow of that dilapidated hay barn that I realized that I wasn't in the wrong place at the wrong time all those years. I was right where God had planted me all along. He moved me out there for a time and then He moved me on when my work there was done. It was comforting to know God had a plan for me. In the meantime, the rain had stopped and a pale rainbow had formed just over the barn. A beam of sunshine fell from the sky and seemed to confirm my new convictions.

I picked up the bridle and coveralls, hung them back in their rightful place and walked over to my car. A hunk of old rotten binder twine caught my shoe and I squatted down, picked it up, rolled it in a ball and threw it in the back seat. Handy stuff, that binder twine. You never know when you're going to need some. I slid into the driver's seat, fired up the engine and drove down the lane. The time had come for me to move out, move up and move on.

Hmmmm, movin' out, movin' up 'n movin' on,
might be a good name for the next book...

As I was gettin' together the next twenty-five
of my farmer's daughter's stories,
I was thinkin' you might have a few homegrown
"laugh-'til-you-cry-stories" you'd like to share.
If you do, visit www.dddunn.com and tell me about it.
I'd love to hear from you and
maybe we can even get your story in a future
Homegrown Humor From The Heartland.

If you are up for an hour or so of
laughin' 'til your cheeks hurt,
schedule a personal appearance for a reading,
key-note, book signing or other get-together.
You can reach me at Bindertwine@dddunn.com.

BOOK ORDER FORM

Name ____

Organization ______________________________________

Address ❑ Work ❑ Home ____________________________

City ______________________ State ______ Zip ______

Home Phone ______________ Work __________________

Fax ____________________ Website ________________

Email ____

Quantity ordering __________ x $9.95 = $__________

WI sales tax: add 5.5% = $__________

Shipping and Handling—First Book $4.50 = $__________

Additional Books—Shipping and Handling—per book $1.00 = $__________

ISBN: 0-9647663-2-9

TOTAL $__________

All orders pre-paid please!

❑ By credit card: ❑ VISA ❑ MasterCard ❑ AMEX

Card #: ________ - ________ - ________ - ________

Expiration Date: _____ Signature ________________________

❑ By check: Payable to **Goblin Fern Press, Inc.**
3809 Mineral Point Road
Madison, WI 53705

Orders may be submitted by mail, fax or through our secure website, **www.goblinfernpress.com**.

Toll-free: 888-670-BOOK (2665) • Email: info@goblinfernpress.com

Tel: 608-442-0212 • Fax: 608-442-0221